STERLING BIOGRAPHIES®

ALEXANDER HAMILTON

His Life, Our History

By Susan Blackaby

STERLING CHILDREN'S BOOKS
New York

To the enduring memory of Miss Ablard,
Jordan Junior High, Palo Alto, 1966

STERLING CHILDREN'S BOOKS
New York

An Imprint of Sterling Publishing Co., Inc.
1166 Avenue of the Americas
New York, NY 10036

ISBN 978-1-4549-2869-0

Distributed in Canada by Sterling Publishing Co., Inc.
c/o Canadian Manda Group, 664 Annette Street
Toronto, Ontario M6S 2C8, Canada
Distributed in the United Kingdom by GMC Distribution Services
Castle Place, 166 High Street, Lewes, East Sussex BN7 1XU, England
Distributed in Australia by NewSouth Books
45 Beach Street, Coogee, NSW 2034, Australia

For information about custom editions, special sales, and premium and
corporate purchases, please contact Sterling Special Sales at 800-805-5489
or specialsales@sterlingpublishing.com.

Manufactured in China

Lot #:
2 4 6 8 10 9 7 5 3 1
10/18

sterlingpublishing.com

For image credits, see page 181

Cover image courtesy of Wikimedia Commons/Bureau of Engraving and Printing

Cover and interior design by Irene Vandervoort

Contents

Events in the Life of Alexander Hamilton

1755

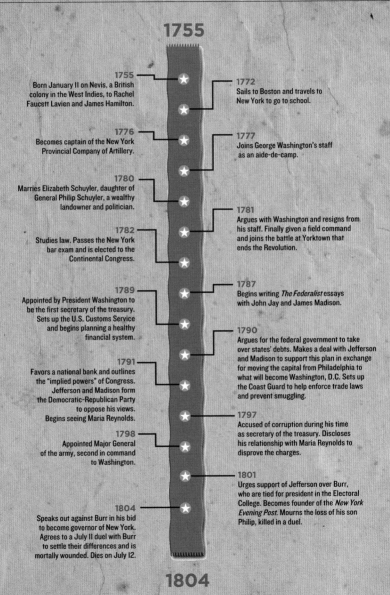

1755
Born January 11 on Nevis, a British colony in the West Indies, to Rachel Faucett Lavien and James Hamilton.

1772
Sails to Boston and travels to New York to go to school.

1776
Becomes captain of the New York Provincial Company of Artillery.

1777
Joins George Washington's staff as an aide-de-camp.

1780
Marries Elizabeth Schuyler, daughter of General Philip Schuyler, a wealthy landowner and politician.

1781
Argues with Washington and resigns from his staff. Finally given a field command and joins the battle at Yorktown that ends the Revolution.

1782
Studies law. Passes the New York bar exam and is elected to the Continental Congress.

1787
Begins writing *The Federalist* essays with John Jay and James Madison.

1789
Appointed by President Washington to be the first secretary of the treasury. Sets up the U.S. Customs Service and begins planning a healthy financial system.

1790
Argues for the federal government to take over states' debts. Makes a deal with Jefferson and Madison to support this plan in exchange for moving the capital from Philadelphia to what will become Washington, D.C. Sets up the Coast Guard to help enforce trade laws and prevent smuggling.

1791
Favors a national bank and outlines the "implied powers" of Congress. Jefferson and Madison form the Democratic-Republican Party to oppose his views. Begins seeing Maria Reynolds.

1797
Accused of corruption during his time as secretary of the treasury. Discloses his relationship with Maria Reynolds to disprove the charges.

1798
Appointed Major General of the army, second in command to Washington.

1801
Urges support of Jefferson over Burr, who are tied for president in the Electoral College. Becomes founder of the *New York Evening Post*. Mourns the loss of his son Philip, killed in a duel.

1804
Speaks out against Burr in his bid to become governor of New York. Agrees to a July 11 duel with Burr to settle their differences and is mortally wounded. Dies on July 12.

1804

A Man Named Hamilton

Mine is an odd destiny.
— *Letter to Gouverneur Morris, February 29, 1802*

Who Was Alexander Hamilton?

This seems like a simple question. If you're looking for hashtags, the labels that describe Hamilton include #orphan, #clerk, #student, #patriot, #soldier, #lawyer, #FoundingFather, #nation-builder, and #statesman.

But there's more.

Hamilton was smart. He brought a lot of talent to every task. He stored up experiences. He examined details. He put ideas together in new ways.

Hamilton was a careful planner. He weighed his options. He went after advantages. He set a course for greatness.

Hamilton was a hard worker. He got results by mixing time with purpose.

Hamilton was a fantastic communicator. His words on paper and at the podium forged the future.

Hamilton could be weak. He could be thoughtless. He could be foolish. He could be proud and stubborn. In short, he could be just like anyone else.

But above all, Alexander Hamilton was a perfect example of the American dream. Armed with courage, Hamilton tackled opportunities with confidence. He aimed high. He wanted to succeed.

Alexander Hamilton was a key player in the politics of colonial America. His foresight and wisdom helped the Founding Fathers form "a more perfect Union." He influenced the ideas, decisions, arguments, and events that created the new nation and sustain it to this day.

CHAPTER 1

Beginnings

It seems my birth is the subject of the most humiliating criticism.

—Letter from Hamilton to William Jackson, August 26, 1800

Alexander Hamilton was born January 11, 1755, on the Caribbean island of Nevis. His father, James Hamilton, came from a well-to-do family in Scotland. James grew up in the comfortable surroundings of a large country estate called the Grange.

This is the Hamilton family coat of arms.

According to English law, only the firstborn son could inherit property. James was the fourth son of nine. He could not depend on his family's wealth for support. He needed somehow to make his own way. He set off to find a new life for himself. He wound up in the plantations of the West Indies.

The West Indies

The West Indies was once a mountain range that is now mostly covered by water. The ancient peaks form an island chain that stretches over 2,000 miles. Thousands of islands separate the Gulf of Mexico and Caribbean Sea from the Atlantic. The islands, which belong to many different nations, are divided into groups. Nevis, St. Kitts, and St. Croix are a cluster of islands in the Caribbean. They are part of the Leeward Islands in the Lesser Antilles—"lesser" because they are small.

The tiny islands of the West Indies could mean huge profits for landowners, traders, and merchants. They had the perfect climate to grow the sugarcane that sweetened every cup of tea in Europe.

Unfortunately, James Hamilton was lazy and distracted. He had no head for business, which put any hope of success well beyond his reach. He was, however, handsome and lighthearted. His charm made his shortcomings easier to overlook.

A Hasty Escape

Alexander Hamilton's mother was Rachel Faucett Lavien. She met Alexander's father, James, around 1750. At the time, she was on the run from a very bad marriage. Rachel's husband, Johann Lavien, had married her for her youth, her beauty, and, more to the point, her inheritance. Rachel's money paid for their small sugar plantation on the Danish island of St. Croix. She and Lavien soon had a son named Peter.

It was not possible to "get rich quick" by owning a plantation. Turning a profit took a lot of time and a lot of money. Fortune hunters such as Johann Lavien often ran out of both before they found success.

It was not long before the Laviens suffered a series of disastrous setbacks. By the time the money and the land disappeared, the unhappy marriage was all but over. Rachel tried to take her son and leave, but the bitter and abusive Lavien stopped her. He accused her of being a "shameless, rude, and ungodly" wife and had her arrested. Lavien had the full force of Danish law on his side. Getting locked in a dungeon for a few months was meant to teach Rachel a lesson. She was expected to settle down and obey her husband. She may have promised to cooperate with Lavien in exchange for her freedom. However, once released from jail, Rachel needed to get away in order to survive. It was a heartbreaking choice, but she left her son behind. She sailed to St. Kitts to start her life over again.

The Faucett Family

Rachel Faucett's successful and respected family had been on the island of Nevis since the late 1600s. The Faucetts maintained both a sugarcane plantation and a home in the capital. Rachel's father was a scholar and a gentleman. He ran the plantation and also became a physician. Against the backdrop of the blue Caribbean, Rachel had enjoyed a rich and privileged upbringing. When her father died, he left all of his assets to her—the legacy soon squandered by Johann Lavien.

The Hamiltons

Soon after Rachel's arrival in St. Kitts, she met James Hamilton. They began living together as husband and wife and presented themselves as a married couple. This was not unusual at the time. English common law required them to live together for seven years in order to be considered married. This may have been what James intended. It is not clear how much he knew about Rachel's past.

Rachel was bright and well educated, organized and industrious. She poured her energy into trying to help James stay afloat through one failure after another. Once her two sons were born—James Jr. in 1753 and Alexander in 1755—Rachel devoted herself to keeping the family together.

Of the two boys, Alexander was quick-witted and curious. Because the church did not recognize their parents' common law marriage, the boys weren't welcome at the Christian school. For a short time, they attended the Jewish academy on Nevis. Alexander could recite the Ten Commandments in Hebrew when he was only five years old. Otherwise the boys were tutored and homeschooled as their father hopped the family from island to island and job to job. Rachel used books from her library to instruct Alexander, and she taught him to speak French.

Disgrace, Defeat, Death

On a trip back to St. Croix from St. Kitts in 1765, Rachel's unlucky past caught up with her. She found out that Johann Lavien had been granted a divorce back in 1759.

News did not travel fast from island to island. Johann Lavien wanted to remarry and filed for divorce at the court on St. Croix. Rachel did not know about the hearing and was not on hand to stand up for her rights.

According to the terms of the settlement, Rachel was never allowed to get married again. In keeping with the times, Lavien's extreme action branded Rachel as an adultress and her sons as illegitimate. It is easy to see how this stunning news caused problems between Rachel and James. Although the finer points are unknown, the fallout is clear: within a few months, James Hamilton returned to St. Kitts alone. Alexander, who was then ten years old, assumed that the family would one day be reunited.

Over the years, he reached out to try to stay in touch with his father, but they never saw each other again.

Rachel suddenly found herself alone with two young sons to support. She fell back on business skills that James could never seem to master, and she opened a small store. She sold basic goods to planters and ship captains who worked for Beekman and Cruger, a trading firm out of New York. Alexander worked alongside his mother as her assistant. She taught him how to tend to customers, fill orders, handle money, keep track of the inventory, and enter accounts.

It took a couple of years for Rachel's hard work and determination to begin to pay off, but she was smart and she was careful. In January of 1768, Alexander turned thirteen, and the future seemed bright. But by February, that vision of the future had ended. Rachel and Alexander both came down with yellow fever. Alexander recovered; Rachel died.

Yellow Fever

Yellow fever is a virus spread from person to person by infected mosquitoes. Its origins can be traced to Africa. It likely traveled to the Americas during the slave trade. Symptoms include chills, fever, headache, muscle pain, and nausea. Its effect on liver function makes the skin turn yellow, which is where it gets its name.

Most cases of yellow fever are mild, but severe cases can lead to serious and sometimes fatal complications. Today, yellow fever is kept in check with vaccines. In Hamilton's day, doctors did not really understand the disease. For many patients, including Rachel, the treatment did more harm than the fever itself.

Because the law did not recognize Alexander and James Jr., they could not inherit their mother's estate. Rachel's firstborn son, Peter Lavien, claimed the small amount of money and few belongings Rachel had. He did not, however, get her library. Rachel's brother-in-law bought her collection of books and gave it to Alexander.

Solo

Rachel's family stepped in to help provide for James Jr. and Alexander, now penniless and alone. The boys' older cousin took the orphans into his household. He was a struggling merchant with a complicated family life and an unstable personality. Within a year, tragedy struck again. The cousin committed suicide. He didn't leave any instructions for James Jr. and Alexander's welfare.

With this last fracture, the Hamilton brothers went their separate ways. James Jr. shared his father's lack of business sense. He needed to learn a trade, so he signed on to train with a carpenter. Alexander had already taken a job with Beekman and Cruger, the trading company connected to his mother's business. He worked as a clerk in the St. Croix office. Alexander was still too young to live on his own. He moved in with the family of his best friend, Ned Stevens. Ned's father was a wealthy merchant. His influence and connections would help shape Alexander's future.

The instability, uncertainty, betrayal, and sorrow of Alexander's childhood left their mark. He never forgot the private pain of loss and suffering. He never escaped the undeserved public shame caused by his mother's tough choices and his father's failings.

But he tried.

Even as his life crumbled around him, Alexander took steps to overcome his misfortunes and put his nimble intellect to work. After all that had happened to him, what did he have to lose?

Nothing.

CHAPTER 2

The Counting House

I wish there was a war.

— *Letter to Ned Stevens, November 11, 1769*

A lexander was just thirteen when he went to work for Beekman and Cruger in 1768. At that time, the tiny island of St. Croix was home to landowners and fortune hunters, managers and merchants, traders and outlaws, sailors and scalawags, and thousands and thousands of enslaved people. The Danish government controlled the waterfront. More than 1,000 vessels came and went each year—a lot of traffic in one little port!

Christiansted was the capital of St. Croix. It included a fort, customs house, church, warehouses, and government buildings.

Beekman and Cruger was one of the busiest and most successful shipping firms. It had offices in New York and London, connections in West Africa, and counting houses at ports throughout the Caribbean. Nicholas Cruger was just twenty-five when he arrived in St. Croix from the main office in Manhattan. He hired Alexander—the small, sharp, energetic orphan kid—to assist him.

On-the-Job Training

Alexander worked in Cruger's counting house instead of going to school. Abilities that would have helped him in the classroom turned out to be just as useful on the job. Again and again, Alexander proved himself to be extraordinarily gifted, disciplined, and organized. He was a quick study and a tireless employee, which worked out well; being a

Nicholas Cruger was one of the first people to recognize that Alexander was no ordinary wharf waif.

clerk at Beekman and Cruger gave Alexander plenty to learn and plenty to do.

Alexander's duties put him at the heart of the global economy. To figure out international pricing, he calculated exchange rates between different currencies. To schedule and chart safe shipping routes, he watched weather patterns and tides. To estimate shipments, he had to understand how much each type of vessel could hold. To manage shipments, he had to know how best to load and unload cargo. To supply provisions to the nearly 400 plantations on the island, he tracked planting and harvesting seasons. Besides these tasks, Alexander kept the books up to date and wrote business letters.

As ships arrived in port, Alexander inspected the dizzying variety of freight loaded and offloaded every day. Most of the available land on St. Croix was set aside for growing sugarcane. This didn't leave much room for growing other crops or raising livestock. Everything the population needed in order to survive had to be shipped in from somewhere else. Brokers exported white and brown sugar, molasses, and rum. They imported food, clothing, building materials, mules, cows, and laborers.

Sugar production required many hands doing difficult jobs under terrible conditions. In the early 1800s there were 30,000 people living on St. Croix; 26,500 of them were enslaved.

The Slave Trade

The plantation economy was based on using enslaved people to provide the workforce. These men, women, and children were kidnapped from West African villages. The voyage to the West Indies could take up to three months. Many of the captives died on the way. Others managed to escape when they reached port. The rest were sold to plantation owners.

Life for enslaved people was a daily struggle. They endured illnesses, accidents, dangerous working conditions, and horrific treatment. Only the very strongest could survive more than about five years in the sugarcane fields.

The Middle Passage

Trade routes between Europe, Africa, and the New World moved raw materials, manufactured goods, and human cargo across the Atlantic. The slave trade between West Africa and the sugarcane fields of the Caribbean islands and tobacco and cotton plantations of the American South was called the Middle Passage.

In St. Croix, Alexander Hamilton was an eyewitness to what he considered to be the vicious inhumanity of slavery: the extraordinary suffering of the people forced to make the journey; the callous indifference of the traders in the marketplace; the extreme cruelty of the slaveholders and overseers; and the backbreaking brutality of the work. His experiences informed his opinions. He spent his life speaking out in favor of abolition and emancipation—ideas that were decades ahead of their time. By the early 1800s, the transatlantic slave trade ended, but it took many more years for slavery itself to be abolished.

Getting Restless

Alexander was perfectly suited to the varied challenges of his job, but the better he performed, the more frustrated he became. He could see the wide gap between rich and poor on St. Croix. Without a foundation of money and influence, how far would talent and knack take him? Building skills for a way out required finding a way to stand out.

Alexander came to believe that bravery in battle could be his only chance to climb higher than a clerk's perch in a counting house. He shared this belief with his friend Ned, who was now studying medicine in New York City.

Alexander addressed this envelope to his friend Ned in New York.

"[I] would willingly risk my life tho' not my Character to exalt my Station."

Alexander wanted a conflict and the chance to prove himself.

A Leg Up

While he dreamed of glory on the battlefield, Alexander looked for other ways to get noticed. He caught his first unexpected break when he was sixteen. Alexander's boss, Nicholas Cruger, got sick in the fall of 1771. Cruger sailed for New York City and left Alexander in charge of the St. Croix office.

Did this unsupervised power go to Alexander's head? Yes.

Alexander immediately took full advantage of Cruger's absence. He spoke as Cruger's representative and acted with his authority. In his own name but on Cruger's behalf, Alexander wrote to influential people who did business with the firm. He hoped his letters would create a lasting impression.

Alexander fully understood the firm's day-to-day operations. He was able to make quick, sound decisions with steady confidence. He was in charge of people much older than he was, but he did not let their age or experience intimidate him. He called out their mistakes and summarized their shortcomings. The scolding could be snide—"Reflect continually on the unfortunate voyage you have just made"—and the reports sent to the New York office could be scornful—"His cargo was stowed very hickledy-pickledy."

Alexander's management style may have been heavy-handed, and he certainly took liberties with the responsibility he had been given. However, he got results. When Cruger returned to St. Croix six months later, outstanding debts had been collected. Daily operations in port were streamlined. Profits were solid. Cruger owed the survival of his business to Alexander's effort and ability.

Free Time and Free Will

With Cruger back in charge, Alexander resumed his previous duties. In his spare time he drilled with the local **militia**—a fighting force trained to help the regular army in an emergency. He also attended meetings led by Hugh Knox, a forward-thinking Presbyterian minister. Knox preached the power of free will. He urged Alexander to look beyond the limits of his background. Knox believed that the strength of hard work and education could overcome any barriers. He helped Alexander see that there could be a way for him to escape. Knox became Alexander's teacher and advocate. He introduced Alexander to new subjects and new opportunities.

In addition to his mother's books, Alexander used Knox's extensive library to study Shakespeare's plays, Greek philosophy and poetry, and the histories of Roman statesmen. He also spent time writing. He submitted poems to the island newspaper to boost his name recognition among people in the upper class. And mostly he waited for another break.

A Turning Point

Alexander's second break blew in on August 31, 1772. That night, a tremendous hurricane swept across the island of St. Croix. Battering wind and drenching rain caused widespread damage.

Alexander wrote an account of the storm in a letter to his father. Knox submitted the letter for publication. Alexander's vivid description of the storm's destruction got a lot of attention. Island residents in a position to help Alexander succeed joined with Knox and Cruger to raise money for his education. Anyone who met Alexander could readily see his potential. He was a bright kid. He deserved a bright future.

Alexander's mentors quickly made arrangements for him to attend school in the colonies. They assumed that he would follow his friend Ned into medicine. They expected him to settle back in St. Croix once he earned his degree, and that may have been his plan. Taking the chance of a lifetime, Alexander set sail. He left the sorrows of his past behind him.

And he never returned.

The Hurricane

It began about dusk, at North, and raged very violently till ten o'clock. Then ensued a sudden and unexpected interval, which lasted about an hour. Meanwhile the wind was shifting round to the South West point, from whence it returned with redoubled fury and continued so 'till near three o'clock in the morning. Good God! what horror and destruction. It's impossible for me to describe or you to form any idea of it. It seemed as if a total dissolution of nature was taking place. The roaring of the sea and wind, fiery meteors flying about it in the air, the prodigious glare of almost perpetual lightning, the crash of the falling houses, and the ear-piercing shrieks of the distressed, were sufficient to strike astonishment into Angels.

—Excerpt from article printed in the *Royal Danish American Gazette*, St. Croix, October 3, 1772

CHAPTER 3

America

Then join hand in hand, brave Americans all,
By uniting we stand, by dividing we fall;
In so righteous a cause let us hope to succeed,
For heaven approves of each generous deed.

— *"The Liberty Song" by John Dickinson, 1768*

At the end of October 1772, Alexander Hamilton left St. Croix to begin his studies in New York. His first stop was Boston, where he found himself surrounded by a hubbub of unrest. Frustration with the British government had been growing for years, and tempers were short. British soldiers occupied the city. They patrolled the streets to keep the colonists in line.

The Sons of Liberty

At the heart of the fight to protect colonists' rights was a group called the Sons of Liberty. These patriots met in secret. They shared information and ideas. They planned protests against unfair laws, taxes, and **tariffs**. The organization got its start in Boston in 1765. Before long, the network had spread throughout the colonies. By the time Hamilton arrived in America, the Sons of Liberty held protests in every major city.

In Boston, public demonstrations against British policies often turned violent. The British had been forced to cancel the Stamp Act, a tax on printed paper. They pushed back by charging the colonists fees on glass, lead, paper, paint, and tea. To make their point, they set up a customs house in Boston to collect payments owed to the government. They anchored warships in the harbor to enforce the rules. All of these actions made the Boston patriots mad.

The Stamp Act

The French and Indian War was a nine-year conflict between Britain and France. It finally ended in 1763. Victory gave the British control of North America. Before the war, Britain honored the many separate agreements and treaties it had set up with each individual colony. After the war, Britain needed money. In 1765, British Parliament voted to pass the Stamp Act. This

was the first direct tax imposed on all thirteen colonies with one stroke of the pen. It charged all American colonists a tax on every piece of printed paper they used. Stamped pages showed proof of payment.

Colonists saw the Stamp Act as a threat to their rights and freedoms. **Parliament** ignored letters of protest from governing bodies in each colony. It refused to address colonists' complaints. Without a platform to discuss issues, the colonists took action instead. They boycotted British goods. When British merchants in the colonies started going out of business, Parliament was forced to give in. It repealed the Stamp Act but imposed even harsher taxes and trade barriers. In the colonies, these actions planted seeds of distrust and discontent. They would soon start to grow.

The Sons of Liberty wrote letters of protest outlining their complaints to keep the public informed. The letters were published in newspapers and posted in taverns. During his

short stay in Boston, Hamilton read an argument demanding the right of Bostonians to choose their own governor and judges. He went to the rally and watched the angry crowd march through the streets.

The war that Hamilton dreamed of was right around the corner.

The Arrival

Hamilton stayed a few days in Boston and then traveled on to New York City. People sharing the stagecoach with him would have seen a slight boy of seventeen with bright violet-blue eyes and sandy-colored hair. They would have seen a kid ready to start a whole new life.

This drawing shows Hamilton on his eighteenth birthday, shortly after he arrived in New York.

The journey through New England on the Post Road took a week. Hamilton arrived in New York City and knocked on Ned Stevens's door. Ned lived near King's College, overlooking the Hudson River.

Hamilton's first errand was to check in with his employers at Cruger's main office. There he met Hercules Mulligan, who became a lifelong friend. Mulligan was a tailor who specialized in high-end goods. He counted some of the wealthiest and most important men in Manhattan among his customers. He was selected to be Hamilton's guardian and took charge of the money Cruger gave Hamilton for his allowance.

Hercules Mulligan

Hercules Mulligan was a big man with a big personality. He always dressed with care and elegance. He was a walking advertisement for the quality of the clothing he made. Mulligan himself was a member of the Sons of Liberty, but anyone with money and good taste was welcome in his shop. His ability to mix easily with pro-British **Loyalists**, British officers, and American patriots would come in handy once war was declared.

Introductions

Mulligan showed Hamilton around New York City and introduced him to Alexander McDougall. McDougall was leader of the Sons of Liberty in New York. He had been arrested and jailed for his writings against Britain. His courage to speak out in support of the American cause impressed Hamilton. Hamilton may have decided then and there to join the patriots, but he wasn't ready to take sides. School came first.

THE THIRTEEN COLONIES

Beginning in the late 1500s, people wanting to stake claims in the New World sailed across the Atlantic. In most cases, the Crown gave individual leaders or corporations permission to establish settlements.

Who would move across the ocean to an unknown future? Some people had a spirit of adventure. Some wanted religious freedom. Some wanted to make money. Settlements grew, and people who agreed with each other banded together. In time the settlements became distinct colonies. Each one had cities and towns, ports and roads, rules and regulations.

At first, Britain did not bother the people carving out new lives in America. Colonists were left alone to govern themselves as long as they upheld the laws of the homeland. Later, when Britain decided to tap the colonies for cash, the colonists resented the interference. They had come to believe that they had a right to make their own decisions. The British Parliament disagreed.

Hamilton had a letter of recommendation from Hugh Knox to give to the board of trustees at Princeton. Princeton was the Presbyterian college in New Jersey. Mulligan arranged a meeting to discuss Hamilton's future. At the meeting, Hamilton found out he needed more education in a hurry. He had never studied Latin or Greek language and, in spite of his years of bookkeeping, his math skills were terrible. He couldn't get into Princeton without passing those classes. The problem was that he didn't have enough funding to stay in New York and hire a tutor. The solution was to enroll at Elizabethtown Academy in New Jersey. It was one of the best schools in America, and Hamilton could study there at his own pace.

Mulligan sailed with Hamilton across the Hudson River and helped get him settled in New Jersey. Mulligan's well-connected friends were immediately drawn to Hamilton and sensed something special about him. Two lawyers in particular, Elias Boudinot and William Livingston, welcomed him into their homes and let him stay rent-free. Their interest and encouragement started Hamilton on his path to becoming one of the most important men in American history.

William Livingston (1723–1790) spoke out in favor of the Revolution, was a delegate to the First Continental Congress, and served as the first governor of New Jersey.

New Jersey

Hamilton threw himself into his classes. He had a lot to prove and no time to

waste. He had his books open by six in the morning and studied late into the night. He could often be seen outdoors, pacing as he recited Greek and Latin lessons aloud. Plenty of people made fun of this habit, but it was the method Hamilton used throughout his life to understand and absorb information. Reading aloud helped Hamilton organize his thoughts, and he could quickly cover a huge amount of material. Hamilton worked hard to grasp ideas and build his knowledge. It helped to be smart, but Hamilton was a study machine.

Hamilton spent his scant free time with the Livingstons and Boudinots. He enjoyed joining their family gatherings. At their stately homes they hosted the serious movers and shakers of American politics. Hamilton met many future leaders, officers, and statesmen. This rootless student from the West Indies impressed the guests. He carried himself like a gentleman. He discussed issues with insight and depth. He made clever conversation. He delighted their daughters.

Applying to College

Hamilton completed three years' worth of college prep classes in just one year. His tutors were amazed by his determination and ability. He chose to apply to Princeton because the college spoke out against the British Parliament's abuse of power. Admission seemed certain.

Hamilton passed the examination without any trouble and was all but in. It was then that he asked permission to speed up his studies so that he could finish as quickly as possible. This proposal was not unreasonable. Students in those days started college at sixteen. At almost nineteen, Hamilton was older than the other beginning students. He was anxious to make up for lost time. He also didn't want his money to run out. His request needed to be approved by the trustees. Hamilton left the meeting assuming he would be admitted. After all, many of the college trustees knew and admired him.

Two weeks later, Hamilton received a rejection letter.

Hamilton was surprised and disappointed, but he buried his feelings and moved on. He applied to King's College, again asking to study at his own pace. The college accepted him and agreed to his terms. In the fall of 1773, Hamilton loaded his books into a trunk and moved back across the Hudson to New York City.

What happened at Princeton?

Years later, Hercules Mulligan still wondered about the Princeton rejection. Did anyone even ask the trustees to consider Hamilton's request? Probably not. Livingston and Boudinot pulled the strings at Princeton. They were among Hamilton's strongest supporters and closest friends. It is hard to imagine why they would object to his request. Did Princeton reject Hamilton because of his background? Very likely. Hamilton may have been a promising young man, but that didn't make up for the fact that he was illegitimate. The college upheld a strict moral code, and there were no exceptions.

CHAPTER 4

Student to Soldier

No man in his senses can hesitate in choosing to be free, rather than a slave.

> —*Alexander Hamilton*, A Full Vindication of the Measures of the Congress, 1774

Without missing a beat, Hamilton rejoined the rowdy racket of New York City. Hamilton had enjoyed the quiet life among New Jersey gentlemen, but he felt more at home in the busy crush of Manhattan's streets. New York brought together people of all backgrounds, from free people who formerly had been enslaved, to the British elite. It was a place where an orphan from a speck in a tropical sea could rise above his rocky start—or in spite of it.

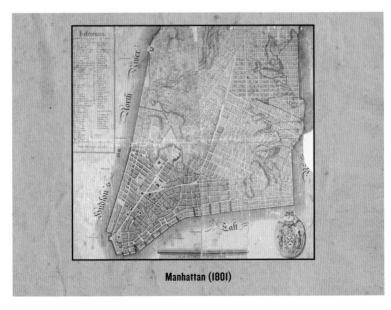

Manhattan (1801)

Financial District

■ See and Do

1. New York Stock Exchange
2. 23 Wall Street
3. Trump Building
4. Federal Hall
5. Trinity Church
6. Bowling Green
7. National September 11 Memorial
8. One World Trade Center
9. St Paul's Chapel
10. Woolworth Building
11. New York by Gehry
12. City Hall
13. Manhattan Municipal Building
14. African Burial Ground Ntnl. Monument
15. Museum of American Finance
16. Museum of Jewish Heritage
17. National Museum of the American Indian
18. New York City Police Museum
19. Skyscraper Museum
20. South Street Seaport Museum

■ Eat

1. Terry's

■ Buy

1. Century 21
2. World Financial Center

■ Sleep

1. Andaz Wall Street
2. Conrad New York
3. Eurostars Wall Street
4. Gild Hall
5. Holiday Inn Wall Street
6. Millenium Hilton
7. New York Marriott Downtown

Manhattan (present day)

Manhattan

New York City in 1773 was one of the largest towns in America. It hugged the lower tip of Manhattan, surrounded by water on three sides. Docks, shipyards, warehouses, homes, shops, churches, taverns, and 25,000 people occupied the space of one square mile—roughly from Battery Park to Chambers Street on today's map. A short ride up Broadway led right out of town. From there, huge manor houses belonging to the upper crust dotted the countryside. Beyond them stretched farms, fields, and forests.

Back to School

Mulligan dropped Hamilton off at the student quarters. Mulligan had attended King's College and was glad that Hamilton would be close by. For Hamilton, being at King's presented a chance to consider both sides of the conflict brewing in the colonies. King's was the only college that supported the Crown. Outside the gates of King's, the Sons of Liberty lashed out as the British clamped down on the colonists. Inside the gates of King's, professors and clergy who were **Tories**—the name given to those in favor of British rule—improved minds and manners. Students kept to a demanding schedule and followed strict rules. Consequences inspired Hamilton to stay out of trouble. Students who broke the rules paid steep fines; students who followed the rules got to spend that money on books. Still, debates could be heated and lively. Many of Hamilton's fellow classmates came from Loyalist families who supported British interests.

Hamilton went back to his tried-and-true study routine. On nice days, he paced the campus, reading aloud and talking to himself. He spent hours in the library, working on assignments. He read history books. He pored over political writings. He studied biographies of world leaders. As a pre-med student, he took classes in anatomy. He also still needed help with math. Hamilton was lucky enough to meet a math tutor with a hands-on teaching method. Robert Harpur used currency exchange, interest rates, and discounts to help Hamilton figure percentages. He taught trigonometry by showing Hamilton how to find the arc of a cannonball aimed in a particular direction. Harpur's lessons gave Hamilton critical skills that he would later put to dazzling use.

King's College had been founded by the Church of England. As patriot unrest in New York increased, the college came under fire for its close ties to the British government. Many people had come to the colonies to worship in their own way. They felt that King's College was a threat to religious freedom. It is easy to see why King's would be a target for the anti-British feelings teeming in the streets.

Going Overboard

Hamilton had been at King's College three months when the Sons of Liberty staged the Boston Tea Party. Paul Revere galloped down the Post Road to spread the news. The tension between Britain and the colonies was impossible for anyone to ignore.

The Boston Tea Party

Tea had been taxed in the colonies for years, even after taxes on other goods had been lifted. The Tea Act, passed in 1773, did not add any tax, but it did interfere with trade. The British East India Company was struggling, and Britain gave it a free pass to export tea to the colonies. The set price was lower than from other sources, and the colonial tea traders couldn't compete.

The colonies and Crown had clashed plenty of times over Parliament's right to levy taxes and restrict trade. Tweaking the tea trade was just one more example. In Charleston, Philadelphia, and New York, no one would take delivery of tea from Britain. But British merchants in Boston refused to cave in to patriot pressure. Three East India Company ships arrived in Boston Harbor in late November. Boston patriots demanded that the tea be sent back to England. When the ship captains refused, the patriots took steps to make their point.

On the night of December 16, 1773, a hundred patriots dressed up as Mohawks. They knew they would be recognized, but wearing Native American costumes symbolized their American cause. They boarded the ships and in three hours emptied 342 chests holding forty-five tons of tea into the

harbor. This was not an empty gesture. The reported loss at the time came to £9,659. In today's dollars, the value of that tea would be $1,700,000!

Inspired by the Boston Tea Party, the Sons of Liberty stepped up protests in New York. They threatened harbor pilots and tea traders. They set fire to Governor's House inside Fort George, the headquarters of the British army. The blaze destroyed the building and any records it held that listed the names of radical patriot leaders. A waterfront demonstration meant to echo the Boston Tea Party erupted in violence.

Hamilton later denied being an active member of the Sons of Liberty during this time, though his close friendship with Mulligan and regard for McDougall make that seem unlikely. Even if he did attend the protests, he would have been careful. He risked losing his scholarship or even being expelled if he was known to be involved. Besides that, Hamilton knew how quickly a group could turn into a mob with unpredictable results. He was wary of the chaos he had seen during uprisings in St. Croix. When it came to public demonstrations, he opted to steer clear.

Instead of meeting in the streets, Hamilton started working behind the scenes. He used his talent for writing to put his ideas and influence on paper. In anonymous articles, Hamilton challenged the beliefs held by King's College officials. Unlike the Sons of Liberty, Hamilton recognized King George III's power to rule the British Empire, but

King George III ruled Great Britain and Ireland from 1760 to 1820.

he agreed that it didn't extend to Parliament. When it came to the American colonies, Parliament needed to mind its own business. It did not have the right or the power to make demands on behalf of the king.

Pamphleteer

People did not put their names on the articles and pamphlets they wrote. They wanted readers to be swayed by the ideas instead of by the people expressing them. Hamilton used a number of pen names, including Americus, Monitor, A Friend to America, and Publius. Rumors flew about who had written *A Full Vindication of the Measures of the Congress* and *The Farmer Refuted*, but almost no one believed that Hamilton was the author. How could someone so young express arguments with so much depth and knowledge? Good question.

The British responded to the Boston Tea Party with tighter restrictions and stricter enforcement. Colonists called these new limits The Intolerable Acts because they were simply too much to bear. Patriots in Boston did not appreciate being kept on a short leash, and the rest of the colonists didn't blame them. Everyone had been pushed too far. Patriot leaders began to communicate with each other from colony to colony. It was time to come together in one place for a discussion—something they hadn't ever done before. They called for a Continental Congress to meet in September in Philadelphia.

The Intolerable Acts

Parliament was sick and tired of how the patriots in Boston behaved. After the Boston Tea Party, Parliament set out to teach the colonists in Massachusetts a lesson.

* It closed Boston Harbor until someone paid for the tea.

* It banned all goods coming into the port except for food and firewood.

* It banned town meetings.

* It appointed a new royal governor and increased his power.

* It prevented colonists from trying British troops for murders committed while enforcing British laws.

* It allowed British officers to take over colonists' homes to house their soldiers.

* It granted a big chunk of the Ohio Valley to French-held Quebec. (This was a separate issue but infuriating.)

The punishment being suffered by colonists in Boston drew a mixed response from people in the other colonies. Some believed in keeping the pressure on. They wanted everyone to refuse to do any business with British merchants. Others waffled. They pointed out that making Britain mad ended up hurting everyone. Some said that Boston colonists should just pay for the tea and move on. These opposing viewpoints faced off in choosing **delegates** to attend the Continental Congress. In New York, the more moderate wafflers gained the upper hand. McDougall blew his stack and called a meeting.

On the afternoon of July 6, New Yorkers from all walks of life assembled on the common near King's College. There was a lot of grumbling as McDougall presented reasons for resisting the British and supporting fellow patriots in Boston. When McDougall was shouted down, Hamilton spoke up. He stepped onto the platform and delivered a speech that presented the following points:

- The Boston Tea Party was a patriot victory—for everyone.
- Closing Boston's port was mean-spirited and excessive, even for Britain.
- The colonists needed to show solidarity.
- British taxation was unfair and unreasonable.
- Boycotting British goods was a necessary step.
- The British deserved to get squeezed.

Hamilton wrapped up his speech by saying actions taken against the British would "prove [to be] the salvation of North America and her liberties." The colonists could not let the British triumph over "right, justice, social happiness, and freedom."

The crowd stood in stunned silence.

Who does this kid think he is?

Then it burst into applause.

Alexander Hamilton!

The Continental Congress

When the Continental Congress met, declaring war was not on the agenda. Delegates opened the meeting by stating their loyalty as British subjects. Then they made it clear that they would not be bullied. They formed a Continental Association to completely block British trade. There would be no imports, exports, or use of British goods until Parliament loosened its hold on colonists' liberties. The Intolerable Acts had to go.

Colonies would appoint committee members to police communities to be sure the ban was carried out. New York chose Hercules Mulligan to serve as an enforcer. The meeting closed with a prayer for peace, and the delegates went home.

A War of Words

King's College officials mocked the Continental Congress. They circulated a pamphlet that called the members of the Continental Association "a venomous brood of scorpions." They accused patriots of staging riots to bait the British military into using force, and they spoke out against the trade ban.

Even though Hamilton was a King's College student, this pro-British Tory attack was just the inspiration he needed.

Hamilton responded with a 35-page pamphlet of his own called *A Full Vindication of the Measures of the Congress.* In it he pulled from history, politics, economics, and law. He added stinging insults, witty wisecracks, and biting slights. He cited the British Constitution and quoted philosophers. His arguments pointed out British injustice and fully supported the steps colonists had agreed to take.

Excerpt from
A Full Vindication of the Measures of the Congress

The only distinction between freedom and slavery consists in this: In the former state, a man is governed by the laws to which he has given his consent, either in person, or by his representative: In the latter, he is governed by the will of another. In the one case his life and property are his own, in the other, they depend upon the pleasure of a master. It is easy to discern which of these two states is preferable. **No man in his senses can hesitate in choosing to be free, rather than a slave.**

That Americans are [entitled] to freedom, is [incontestable] upon every rational principle. All men have one common original: they participate in one common nature, and consequently have one common right. No reason can be assigned why one man should exercise any power, or pre-eminence over his fellow creatures more than another; unless they have voluntarily vested him with it. Since then, Americans have not by any act of [theirs empowered] the British Parliament to make laws for them, it follows they can have no just authority to do it.

When the Tories published a rebuttal, Hamilton's next comeback filled 80 pages! Hamilton insisted that the patriots were not calling for war: they just wanted Britain to grant colonists the same liberties that all British subjects enjoyed. In Hamilton's view, the colonists' loyalty was to the king. They simply wished to get out from under Parliament's control. They had not granted Parliament permission to make their laws for them. He wrote: "The sacred rights of mankind are not to be rummaged for among old parchments or musty records. They are written as with a sunbeam, in the whole volume of human nature by the hand of the divinity itself and can never be erased or obscured by mortal power."

The success of Hamilton's speech and the power of his writing put him—and America—on a new path. And Hamilton was just getting warmed up.

CHAPTER 5

Revolution!

Are these the men with which I'm to defend America?

> — *George Washington to his troops, fleeing the battlefield in panic at Kip's Bay, New York, September 15, 1776*

Before the ink was dry on *The Farmer Refuted*, the British took action against Boston's rabble of patriots.

Lexington and Concord

On April 19, 1775, some 700 British Redcoats marched out of Boston. They wanted to take control of a supply of weapons the colonists had stored in Concord. While they were at it, they intended to arrest Boston's most irritating patriot leaders, Sam Adams and John Hancock.

The British plans had been leaked late the night before, and horseback riders—including Paul Revere—fanned out across the countryside, sounding the alarm for colonists to grab their guns and get ready.

In Lexington, the Redcoats were met by the local militia—about eighty armed citizens. Since it was clear that the militia was hopelessly outnumbered, both sides agreed to back down. As the militia left the green, someone started shooting. A short battle left seventeen militiamen dead or wounded.

The Redcoats continued on to Concord. While they searched the town for weapons, militiamen from far and wide quietly gathered at the edge of town. When the Redcoats tried to cross the North Bridge, nearly 400 militiamen opened fire.

Fierce fighting forced the Redcoats to retreat. They started the eighteen-mile march back to Boston. But more than 2,000 militia and Minutemen filled the woods along the route. Snipers crouched behind stone walls and trees and hid behind hedges and sheds, firing at the Redcoats, who were running for their lives. The British suffered heavy losses as the colonists chased them all the way back to Boston.

By the rude bridge that arched the flood
Their flag to April's breeze unfurled,
Here once the embattled farmers stood,
And fired the shot heard round the world.

— from "Concord Hymn," by Ralph Waldo Emerson

The colonists' disorganized and downright devious approach to fighting clearly confused the Redcoats. The British were used to more orderly rules of engagement, with rows of soldiers advancing toward each other across the battlefield. One British officer complained, "What an unfair method of carrying on a war!" Not only did the colonists' tactics throw the Redcoats off balance, they seemed to think they had a shot at winning. This came as unpleasant news to the British.

On April 20, thousands of militiamen surrounded Boston. They were farmers, carpenters, blacksmiths, tailors, wheelwrights, printers, and silversmiths. They stood ready to take on the greatest military might in the world.

The Revolutionary War had begun!

Bugles, fifes, and drums were used to help keep order on the march and send messages on the battlefield. This drum was used by members of the Massachusetts regiment. The motto painted on it is "It is sweet and distinguished to die for one's country."

Engraved for BARNARD's New Complete & Authentic HISTORY of ENGLAND.

Portrait & Uniform of An
AMERICAN GENERAL.

A real representation of the Dress of An
AMERICAN RIFLE-MAN.

Who's Fighting Whom?

The *militia* was a part-time volunteer army. It was made up of citizens trained to defend their colonial towns. Members of the militia were called *militiamen*.

Minutemen were elite forces, so called because they could be "ready in a minute." They were chosen from among the Massachusetts militia for their courage and cunning.

The Americans were called *rebels* after they declared independence.

The Second Continental Congress set up the *Continental Army* in June 1775. It consisted of ten companies of riflemen from Pennsylvania, Maryland, Delaware, and Virginia and forces already in place in Massachusetts and New York. The Congress named George Washington commander-in-chief. These troops were sometimes called *Continentals*.

Redcoats were British soldiers, so called because of their bright red uniforms. British troops were also called *Regulars*.

Joining Up

Within a few days, a horseback rider blazed down the Post Road to bring word of the Revolution to the Sons of Liberty in Manhattan. The patriots went wild. They armed the militia with weapons from the local **arsenal**. Captains took command; men fell into step.

No one was more eager to serve than Alexander Hamilton, and his ambition blasted past his duty. He trained with the other volunteers from King's College every morning before classes. He spent his evenings reading up on military history. He learned everything he could about battle tactics. He also kept up his writing, firing off a series of protest letters for publication.

As the patriots' purpose and organization grew, so did the Tories' fear. Loyalists fled the city, moving their loved ones and belongings to the safety of their country homes. Handbills that circulated blamed the King's College president and his British cronies for the patriot deaths in Lexington and Concord. The handbills carried a warning to the Loyalists: "Fly for your lives or anticipate your doom."

Stalling the Mob

Late on May 10, Hamilton and his roommate woke to the sound of angry shouting at the college gates. Hamilton realized that a patriot crowd was coming after the Tory college president. As Hamilton headed for the front door, he yelled for his classmates to sneak the president out the back way. Four hundred patriots broke through the gate and pushed toward the building. Hamilton met them on the front porch.

Hamilton steeled himself and spoke out. He said that hounding Tories would only hurt the patriots: Do not "disgrace and injure the glorious cause of liberty!" Hamilton's stand delayed the patriots long enough for the president to climb out a window. Barefoot and wearing only a nightshirt, he ran through the dark and soon after sailed for England.

Hamilton held back the mob.

What Was He Thinking?

Hamilton showed cool courage in trying to keep the patriots from storming the college. They had mayhem in mind, which would not have ended well for anyone. At the same time, Hamilton was lucky his actions didn't backfire. There were plenty of patriots who did not understand why Hamilton would go out of his way to protect a Loyalist. But as other incidents have shown, Hamilton could not stand mob violence, even for a cause he supported. As a child, he had seen enslaved people subjected to street violence and brutality. He knew how quickly a crowd could lose control.

Hamilton may have been acting in the heat of the moment as he held back the crowd, but certainly he also realized how much he had to lose by doing so. For one thing, the patriots might have beaten him to a pulp. For another, he was defending a Tory. He risked giving up the respect he had so recently gained as a spokesman for the Sons of Liberty.

Hamilton was all for the Revolution. But he also understood that freedom without any limits could lead to disorder and confusion—which would sooner or later lead to loss of freedom. What tips the balance between liberty and law? Hating an authority is not the same as hating all authority, but the line begins to blur.

Dear Sir

As raids by the Sons of Liberty on Tory businesses increased, Hamilton sent a letter to John Jay. Jay was New York's delegate to the Second Continental Congress, which was meeting in Philadelphia to discuss the war. Hamilton expressed his complaints and concerns: "In times of such commotion as the present, while the passions of men are worked up to an uncommon pitch there is a great danger of fatal extremes." Hamilton suggested that Jay arrange for troops to be sent to New York from Philadelphia and New Jersey to help keep hotheaded mobs in line. Hamilton had met Jay and knew him to be both thoughtful and careful. Jay was likely to agree with Hamilton about the dangers of chasing Tories through the streets.

Hamilton's concern was genuine. But in reaching out to Jay, Hamilton also hoped to get his name into the mix in Congress. Sure enough. Jay asked Hamilton to be his eyes and ears on the street, reporting what the Sons of Liberty were up to in New York. Hamilton's observations included useful information about Loyalist activities, too, since he still had close ties to King's College and Cruger's. Hamilton sent detailed information, and Jay shared it with the other delegates to Congress.

John Jay

Founding Father John Jay practiced law in New York. He was among a group of moderates who wanted change but did not support a complete break from Britain. He hoped Britain and the colonists could reach an agreement without going to war.

Jay was known for being a peacemaker and peacekeeper. He served as the American minister to Spain and secretary of foreign affairs. In building treaties and crafting compromises, he always did what he thought was right—but he did not always do what he was told.

Washington named Jay the first chief justice of the Supreme Court, and he served two terms as governor of New York.

The General

In June 1775, Congress chose George Washington to lead the Continental Army. The Americans had an actual war on their hands, and they were going up against a world-class fighting force. Early victories on the battlefield had been impressive and surprising. The Americans would not win the war without the pluck and purpose of the militia, but they could not win the war without an army.

George Washington was well known and highly respected as a soldier, a landowner, and a statesman when he was chosen to lead the Continental Army. He was forty-three years old.

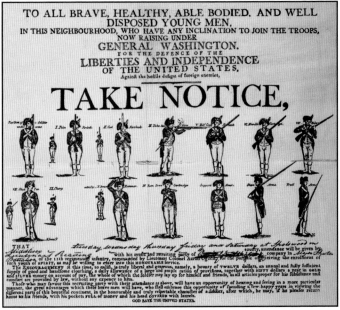

The call went out, urging young men to join Washington's army and "enter into this honorable service."

Washington came from Virginia. Giving him the leadership helped get all of the colonies involved. The fighting had so far been limited to Massachusetts battlefields, but liberty was everybody's cause, not just New England's.

Night Raid

In a final effort to avoid war, Congress drafted the Olive Branch Petition. King George III did not even respond. On August 23, he issued a royal proclamation. The colonists had "proceeded to open and avowed rebellion." The most powerful nation on earth would take on its scruffy colonists and break them once and for all.

On that same night, Alexander Hamilton, Hercules Mulligan, and a dozen other King's College volunteers went down to the Battery below Fort George. They intended to drag twenty-four cannons uptown to City Hall Park to keep them from falling into British hands. As the volunteers started tying ropes to the cannons, the British opened fire. The volunteers managed to haul ten of the heavy guns to safety as **grapeshot** and cannonballs rained down from the British warship anchored offshore. According to Mulligan, Hamilton kept his cool throughout the ordeal and even ran back through the firestorm to fetch his discarded musket. He dodged the British bombardment "with as much unconcern as if the vessel had not been there."

Artillery Command

In March 1776, Hamilton got his scholarship money from Cruger's. He was supposed to use it to pay for his last quarter of college. Instead, he used it to pay Hercules Mulligan to make him a uniform. Hamilton's student days were over. Livingston,

Jay, McDougall, and even Harpur—the math tutor—supported Hamilton's bid to become captain of the New York Provincial Company of Artillery.

Master tailor Mulligan made Captain Hamilton a blue coat with buff cuffs and facings and a pair of white buckskin breeches.

Hamilton's Unit

Hamilton's company still exists as the 1st Battalion 5th Field Artillery Unit and is the oldest unit in the United States Army.

School's Out Forever

King's College closed its doors in April. During the spring and summer, George Washington used the college as a field hospital. When the British captured New York City, they occupied the campus. A fire destroyed most of the buildings later in the war. King's College eventually reopened. It moved about five miles uptown and became Columbia University.

While Hamilton waited for his commission to be approved, his old friend Elias Boudinot asked him to take a promotion and serve as an **aide-de-camp** to Lord Stirling. He was also asked to serve as an aide-de-camp to Nathanael Greene. In both cases, Hamilton would have been the youngest major in the Revolutionary Army and would have had the honor of serving a brilliant commander. These offers may have been both flattering and tempting, but Hamilton had his heart set on glory. He had waited years to prove himself on the battlefield. He wasn't about to give up that chance.

Aide-de-Camp

A military aide-de-camp—or camp helper—serves as an assistant or secretary to a high-ranking officer. It is a position of honor that demands an exceptional level of trust and responsibility. Depending on the people, the relationship, and the circumstances, an aide-de-camp might be asked to give opinions, share ideas, offer advice, and provide support—anything required to get the job done—as well as deliver messages, write out orders, and take care of correspondence and reports.

Getting Results

Being an artillery captain for New York required Hamilton to recruit thirty men to form a company, a tall order. The wages Hamilton could offer were less than the men would get if they joined the Continental Army. Even so, Hamilton and the popular and persuasive Mulligan signed up twenty-five men in just one day. Hamilton plunged into troop training and discipline. His efforts did not go unnoticed. He was quickly able to trade on his leadership and skill to increase troop wages, pay recruiters, add work clothes to the list of critical supplies, and get better rations. Hamilton soon commanded sixty-nine men.

The New York Campaign

After the bloody battles in Boston, troops in New York City knew they would be Britain's next target. Hamilton directed his company in building a fort, one of a series spread across Manhattan from river to river.

King George III did not disappoint.

The British show of military might was meant to scare some sense into the Americans.

On July 2, hundreds of British warships and troop carriers moved into the narrows between Brooklyn and Staten Island. Thousands of British troops disembarked while the Americans watched from Manhattan.

Washington may have felt helpless, considering his ragtag army. The men were barely trained and badly equipped. They were melting down lead peeled from rooftops and windowpanes to build a supply of ammunition. The Americans didn't have a single warship, let alone a fleet.

What did the colonists do, facing 39,000 armed Redcoats? They declared their independence and got ready to fight!

"Free and Independent States"

In Philadelphia, the Continental Congress put the finishing touches on the Declaration of Independence. The resolution passed on July 4.

On July 9, Washington gathered his troops on the common to hear the declaration read aloud. Elated soldiers celebrated by knocking over the statue of King George III in Bowling Green, sending his head rolling.

The colonists were already at war, but they wanted to make sure their reasoning and aims were clear. Colonized people had never before broken away from their mother country to rule themselves, so history was not on their side. What's more, the actions of the

The patriots picked up the scattered parts of the statue and turned the toppled king into 42,088 bullets.

Americans amounted to **treason**, which could be punished by death. No kidding. The humongous British fighting force was ready to carry out the sentence.

Declaration of Independence

Here is the Declaration of Independence as it was written at the time:

IN CONGRESS, JULY 4, 1776

The unanimous Declaration of the thirteen united States of America

When in the Course of human events it becomes necessary for one people to dissolve the political bands which have connected them with another and to assume among the powers of the earth, the separate and equal station to which the Laws of Nature and of Nature's God entitle them, a decent respect to the opinions of mankind requires that they should declare the causes which impel them to the separation.

We hold these truths to be self-evident, that all men are created equal, that they are endowed by their Creator with certain unalienable Rights, that among these are Life, Liberty and the pursuit of Happiness. — That to secure these rights, Governments are instituted among Men, deriving their just powers from the consent of the governed, — That whenever any Form of Government becomes destructive of these ends, it is the Right of the People to alter or to abolish it, and to institute new Government, laying its foundation on such principles and organizing its powers in such form, as to them shall seem most likely to effect their Safety and Happiness.

The Fall of New York

Britain made its first move on July 12. A battleship equipped with forty-four guns and another with twenty-eight sailed up the Hudson, hurling cannonballs at New York City. Hamilton ordered his men to fire from their position on the Battery. One of Hamilton's big cannons backfired, killing a number of his troops. It was a bad way to start.

A few weeks later, Washington's army couldn't hold the line as British troops steamrolled through Brooklyn. The Redcoats had a chance to trap the rebels between the battlefront and the East River. They could have overwhelmed Washington's army and ended the war then and there. Instead, the British took a break. Under the noses of the dozing Redcoats, Washington safely and secretly moved his troops back across to Manhattan.

Before the Americans had a chance to transfer their weapons and supplies, the British barreled back with full force. They attacked the Americans from warships gathered at Kip's Bay on the East River. The ear-splitting noise caused complete confusion and sent the Americans running for cover. Washington zigzagged through the ranks on horseback, shouting at his officers and troops. He cursed the cowardice and chaos as his panicked army bolted for the thick woods north of Manhattan. Hamilton stayed at his post and kept fighting as the Americans retreated. He was one of the last Americans out of the city. He had had to give up his gear and his company's cannons to get away. He was wet and tired and discouraged by the time he reached Harlem Heights at the north end of Manhattan.

The Americans were caught off guard by the power and fury of the British attack.

Meanwhile, the British missed yet another chance to end the war. Instead of chasing down the rebels who were running away, Redcoats flooded into New York City to celebrate their superiority and strength.

Fire!

Once they took over New York City, the Redcoats went to work to reinforce their defenses across northern Manhattan. Then, on a windy night in late September, a blaze broke out in a wooden house by the waterfront. Overnight, 500 buildings—one quarter of the city—turned into smoking rubble. Did stealthy rebels torch the town?

For the next few months, the British continued to outnumber and outgun the rebels. British attacks forced Washington to retreat—from Harlem to White Plains, from New York to New Jersey, from New Jersey to Pennsylvania. The Americans may have lacked reinforcements, food, ammunition, and shoes, but they kept fighting back. Over and over, Hamilton could be heard yelling, "Fire! Fire! Fire!" He directed his gunners with precision and speed to stall the British troops' pursuit, to push back their positions, to stop their progress, to cramp their plans.

George Washington himself noticed Hamilton's "brilliant courage and admirable skill." He sent an aide to find out which commander had helped him safely escape. One of Washington's officers reported seeing Hamilton on the road, "a youth, a mere stripling, small, slender, almost delicate in frame, marching, with a cocked hat pulled down over his eyes, apparently lost in thought, with his hand resting on a cannon, and every now and then patting it, as if it were a favorite horse or a pet plaything."

It was exactly the recognition Hamilton craved.

CHAPTER 6

Promotion

It is not a common Contest we are Ingaged In.

> —*Washington in a letter to Brigadier General William Woodford, March 3, 1777*

The Continental Army had now lost both New York City and New Jersey to the British. Washington ferried his gloomy troops across the Delaware River and once again regrouped. Hamilton and his gunners joined forces along the western bank of the river, firing at British patrols to keep them in check.

As December wore on, winter set in. General Howe, the British commander, got tired of being cold and marched his Redcoats back to New York City. He left behind a company of Hessian soldiers to hold down Trenton.

Instead of being frightened when the Hessians robbed their homes, Trenton colonists became outraged. They responded by harassing the Hessians day and night. One Hessian soldier complained "We have not slept one night in peace since we came to this place." Newly minted rebels made the Hessians' life in Trenton miserable.

Rethinking Strategy

Washington put the December downtime to good use. He was starting to see that the Americans' advantage would be in small-scale skirmishes and raids. Facing the British across a battlefield, the Continental Army barely stood a chance. But Washington's

The Hessians

The British hired 30,000 German troops to help them fight the rebels—one quarter of the British fighting force. Most of these men came from the German state of Hesse-Cassel. All of them were called Hessians.

The Hessian soldiers were highly trained and highly disciplined, and they had a reputation for fearless brutality. They also were well paid. Hessians added to their profits by selling military loot and stealing from civilians.

Hessian units operated under German command, wearing German uniforms and flying the German flag. They showed up with their officers, weapons, and equipment to do a job but otherwise had no stake in the outcome of the conflict. Desertion was not uncommon. At the end of the war, thousands of Hessians stayed behind. They moved to German settlements already established.

troops could do a lot of damage by attacking the rear guard, ambushing patrols, and cutting off retreats. Plus they had the woods and the weather on their side.

Washington sent his spies in all directions to spread false rumors about the Continentals, misrepresenting the size of the army and the abilities of the troops.

Have you heard about Washington's so-called army? A sad collection of clumsy bumblers.

Meanwhile, Washington gathered information to plan a rebel masterstroke in Trenton. He had to act quickly: enlistments were due to expire December 31, and many of his men would head for home.

Victory or Death

Washington gave his men their marching orders on Christmas afternoon. His plan was to attack first thing the following morning. He hoped the groggy Hessians would be sleeping late after their Christmas celebration. The slogan for the battle was "Victory or Death"—there was only one option if the Americans were going to keep their cause alive.

On Christmas night, a storm blew in, bringing wind, sleet, and snow. Just after midnight, Washington and his men loaded equipment, weapons, ammunition, and horses onto barges. They poled across the frigid river and then marched the twelve miles to take up their positions around the outskirts of Trenton.

When they were given the signal, the Americans quickly overran the town. They charged the barracks, holding the Hessians at gunpoint. Hamilton

Washington led his men in a difficult and dangerous attack.

and his gunners were in place to stop any counterattack and prevent a retreat, while Virginia riflemen took the town house by house. The Americans forced the Hessians to surrender. They transported 948 prisoners back across the icy Delaware.

In less than two hours, the Americans defeated one of the strongest fighting forces in the world.

Princeton Revisited

Washington announced follow-up plans to make a move on Princeton on January 2. Soldiers pumped up by the success at Trenton eagerly reenlisted. The rebels showed renewed trust in their commander-in-chief and faith in their ability to get the job done.

The Americans set out in the dead of night for the long march north. Hamilton's gunners wrapped rags around the wheels of the cannons to muffle the noise as they rumbled over the frozen road. At dawn, the advance division arrived at Princeton. It came face to face with a Redcoat brigade brandishing drawn bayonets. The rebels had started to retreat when Washington and a division of Pennsylvania militiamen galloped onto the field, outnumbering and surrounding the British forces. Redcoats on the run took up a position in one of the campus buildings. They started shooting from the windows but could not withstand the double cannon fire Hamilton's gunners hurled at them. Once Hamilton's cannons started blasting, the British surrender came quickly.

Washington was jubilant as he congratulated his troops. "It is a fine fox chase, my boys!"

George Washington rallies his troops to drive the British out of New Jersey.

Did He or Didn't He?

Some accounts of the Battle of Princeton claim that Hamilton aimed a cannon squarely at the college that had rejected him three short years before. Supposedly, the cannonball he fired smashed through a chapel window and bashed into a portrait of King George II.

The modest victories at Trenton and Princeton made a huge difference in changing the course of the war. They boosted American spirits. They kept the British from making a move on nearby Philadelphia. They bought the rebel forces some time. Washington marched his 3,000 troops to Morristown, New Jersey, to set up camp for the winter.

The Fighting Season

The pace of the war picked up or slowed down depending on the time of year. Battles shaped up during the late spring and summer and might extend into the fall. During the early spring, it was too muddy to move troops and equipment around. During the winter, it was too cold and snowy. In the fall, the war wound down, and commanders moved their troops to winter quarters.

Time off was meant to give officers a chance to regroup and relax and soldiers a chance to rest, heal, and train. But life in the winter camp could be bleak when the weather turned severe and supplies ran short.

In spite of hardship and suffering, Washington was able to rally his men. They had the element of surprise on their side when they sneaked through the snow to Trenton in 1776. Who would launch a full-scale attack in the dead of winter? The Americans.

An Unusual War

When it came to war, Britain had plenty of experience, expertise, and success. The American Revolution should have been a piece of cake for them. It wasn't. Here are some reasons why:

* At the time, the army that took the capital city won the war. But the Americans didn't have a capital. When the British claimed New York City, the rebels just moved on, and they could keep moving on from colony to colony to colony.

* Britain had amazing resources. They also had amazing expenses. Everything the British war machine needed—from horses to hay to hats—had to be shipped across the Atlantic, a journey that could take months. They also had to pay for tens of thousands of **mercenaries** hired to join their fighting forces.

* Even small victories helped the Americans rally, building their confidence, strengthening their commitment, and adding to their ranks. With each rebel gain, more militiamen enlisted.

* The British had to take on the expense and manpower of launching attack after attack in battles that they needed to win. The Americans just had to defend themselves and stay out of reach. As long as the Redcoats couldn't capture Washington's army, they couldn't claim victory. As long as the rebels could keep from losing, they could keep wearing down the British forces and using up British resources.

Welcome to the Family

Washington set up his winter headquarters in the tavern on the village green in Morristown, New Jersey. As news of the victories at Trenton and Princeton spread, more volunteers than the Continental Army could handle stepped up to serve. Washington had his hands full. He needed to organize new recruits and lobby Congress for funds. He needed to plan and carry out strategies. He needed to add to his staff. "It is absolutely necessary therefore for me to have persons [who] can think for me as well as execute orders." Washington didn't expect these men to have military skill. "If they can write a good letter, write quick, are methodical and diligent, it is all I expect to find in my aides."

Washington saw Hamilton's talent and awarded him a staff position.

On January 20, Washington invited Hamilton to serve as an aide-de-camp. Washington had seen Hamilton's military skills, he had heard about his writing skills, and he needed someone with strong ties to New York. Hamilton accepted, though it meant losing his chance to be a field commander. Only an offer from the greatest and most powerful leader in America would have made Hamilton give up glory on the battlefield.

For Hamilton, joining "Washington's family," as the general's staff was called, came with a promotion from captain to lieutenant colonel. The lull in the war gave Hamilton time to settle in to his duties and get to know his new boss. Washington and Hamilton worked well together from the start. They built a strong bond of trust and understanding, mutual respect, and single-minded purpose. They made an unbeatable team.

Lieutenant Thomas Thompson

On March 1, Hamilton turned his artillery command over to Lieutenant Thomas Thompson. Thanks to Hamilton's vision and powers of persuasion, Thompson was the first soldier promoted to the rank of officer who had not started out as "a gentleman." Like Hamilton, Thompson did not have family connections or wealth. His promotion to lieutenant was based only on his ability.

Until Hamilton and Thompson came along, no one could rise through the military ranks without money and social standing. Thanks to them, anyone serving in the military can earn a promotion.

The Little Lion

Hamilton served with six staff officers who all shared lodgings at Washington's headquarters. Washington's expectations were strict and exacting. Aides were to have their minds "always upon the stretch, scarce ever unbent, and no hours for recreation." Hamilton was okay with that. He had never spent a lot of time relaxing. In what little spare time he had, Hamilton was glad—as he always had been—to study and read.

For over 1,500 years, the writing tool of choice was a trimmed feather called a quill. Quill pens were used to record some of the most famous and important documents in history, including the Declaration of Independence.

Feathers used to make pens came from particular birds at particular times of the year. Crow, eagle, goose, hawk, owl, swan, and turkey feathers worked well, especially if one of the five outer feathers was plucked in the springtime from the left wing of a living bird. Goose feathers were the most common choice and, for a time, Russian geese supplied Britain with 27 million quills a year! Thomas Jefferson actually raised a special breed of geese so that he would have his own steady supply of pens.

Plucked feathers had to be cured and then trimmed and shaped with a penknife before they could be used—a painstaking, multistep process. Dull pens could be sharpened, but a single quill would not last more than a week—and at the rate Hamilton was writing, the lifespan of his pen would have been far less than that.

A small jar or cup of ink called an inkwell kept a supply of ink handy. Four or five words could be written with one dip of the pen.

Marking a long tradition, quill pens are still placed on counsel tables each day the Supreme Court is in session. Attorneys who argue cases before the Court are given a quill pen and a pewter inkwell that matches a set used by Chief Justice John Marshall. Marshall served on the Supreme Court from 1801 to 1835.

Staff members shared cramped quarters next to Washington's office. The general wanted his aides close by so that he could send for them any time he needed them. They spent long days hunched over portable desks or gathered around small tables, seeing to what Hamilton called "the hurry of business." This could mean writing and copying fifteen or twenty letters a day apiece. Meanwhile, messengers came and went with dispatches, reports, plans, and orders.

The daily routine at headquarters wasn't exactly routine. Washington's habit was to meet with his aides briefly to exchange information and set the tone. From sketchy notes and hasty instructions, aides would compose letters in Washington's name to be sent out with his approval.

Washington didn't waste any time putting Hamilton's writing skills to the test. Hamilton's first letter concerned an urgent and tricky prisoner of war (POW) negotiation. It had to offer diplomatic support but hide the fact that the Continental Congress could not decide on a POW policy. Hamilton's second letter was to tell Major General Gates to get his act together. Troops under his command were deserting over and over so that they could collect the cash bonus when they re-enlisted. His third letter ordered General Benedict Arnold to resist attacking a British garrison in Rhode Island unless he was absolutely positive he could win. All in a day's work!

Hamilton could soon "speak" seamlessly for Washington, sometimes without consulting the general at all. Hamilton understood right away how the general's mind worked and could figure out which issue needed critical and immediate attention. The more Washington relied on Hamilton's abilities and expanded his duties, the more confident Hamilton became.

POW and Spy

After his first assignment as an aide-de-camp, Hamilton went on to become one of the chief players in setting up the exchange of prisoners of war. Hercules Mulligan inspired Hamilton's interest in the POW problem. The British had captured Mulligan during the retreat from Brooklyn Heights. He was free to move about New York City, but he wasn't allowed to leave until he could be traded for a British prisoner of equal rank—or until the war was over.

Mulligan actually escaped in November 1776. He slipped across the Hudson and caught up with Hamilton as the rebels were retreating through New Jersey. Hamilton was amazed and overjoyed to see his friend. But he quickly talked him into going right back to New York City. Mulligan was in a perfect position to gather useful information. He was married to the daughter of a British admiral. He made uniforms for British and Loyalist officers. His brother worked in shipping and could easily keep an eye on troop movements and supplies. As part of Washington's network of spies, the Mulligan brothers were invaluable to the rebel cause.

Washington's staff members faced their demanding job—and Washington's terrible temper—with good-humored camaraderie. Hamilton had an easygoing and agreeable personality, which made him popular with everyone. He built a close circle of friends. Fellow officers appreciated Hamilton's quick wit and entertaining conversation. They did not mind that Hamilton soon became what Washington described as his "principal and most confidential aide." Hamilton was a good egg. Fellow officers called him The Little Lion to describe his fierce enthusiasm both on and off the job.

The Lighter Side

Once in a while Washington's staff earned a break. Hamilton happily joined these celebrations. Martha Washington's visits to the winter camp meant dining, dancing, and merrymaking with the officers' wives and daughters. Hamilton gladly squired ladies around the dance floor and around the town. He charmed them with his banter. He dazzled them with his brilliance. Among his long list of talents, Hamilton was by all accounts a first-class flirt. Martha Washington named her tomcat after him.

"Yes, Your Excellency"

None of the other aides could touch Hamilton's amazing gift with words, but writing was not his only responsibility. Hamilton maintained connections with veteran officers, congressmen, governors, and field commanders. He organized intelligence gathering. He developed political, economic, and military strategies. He streamlined day-to-day operations to define the chain of command. His ability to get things done made Hamilton the general's go-to guy. Washington automatically called on Hamilton first for input and advice. His decision to serve the commander-in-chief proved to be another life-changing opportunity that put Hamilton at the heart of the action.

CHAPTER 7

Trials and Tribulations

For Gods sake, my Dear Sir, exert yourself upon this
occasion, our distress is infinite.

–Letter from Alexander Hamilton to Col. Henry E. Lutterloh,
begging him to supply wagons at Valley Forge, February 1778

In between short blasts of intense action on one battlefield or
another, progress of the war slowed down to a crawl. Moving
troops and equipment from place to place on foot, getting
supplies, and communicating back and forth took up huge
amounts of time, energy, and money. The lack of action and
actual fighting could be frustrating.

Cross Purposes

While the rebels struggled to organize their fighting force,
Congress struggled to organize a government. Delegates in
Philadelphia argued back and forth as they tried to agree on the
Articles of Confederation. A first draft had been presented to
Congress in 1776. Congress then haggled over the details for
months.

Congress agreed on the immediate need to set up a national
government. The states could not coordinate to fight the war if
they did not show some unity. A strong, single sense of purpose
would support the war effort at home and persuade foreign
nations to help out.

Problem: Americans did not like the idea of replacing one form of overreaching power with another. Going forward, each state wanted to keep its land, identity, and ability to rule its citizens. What's more, patriots' hatred of all things King George III included the extensive war machine that he built using their taxes. Over and over, General Washington begged Congress to unite behind the Continental Army to make it bigger and stronger. Over and over, Congress denied his request.

Comrades

Late in the spring of 1777, John Laurens joined Washington's family. Laurens and Hamilton—both twenty-two years old—hit it off immediately. Laurens had only recently returned to America from studies in Europe. He came from a wealthy South Carolina family. He was well connected and well educated. His talents and ambitions mirrored those of Hamilton: sharp-witted, sharp-tongued, dedicated, and determined.

Laurens and Hamilton made a good team that got even better when Gilbert du Motier, the Marquis de Lafayette, arrived from France in August. Deep down, Hamilton was a loner. The losses he had suffered in his young life made him careful about making close connections. But he was able to forge deep

John Laurens became Alexander Hamilton's best friend.

and lasting friendships with both of these amazing young men. Together, Hamilton, Laurens, and Lafayette reflected the spirit of cooperation that built America.

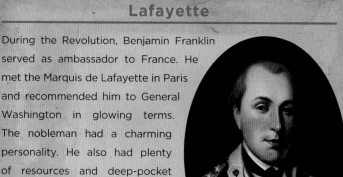

Lafayette

During the Revolution, Benjamin Franklin served as ambassador to France. He met the Marquis de Lafayette in Paris and recommended him to General Washington in glowing terms. The nobleman had a charming personality. He also had plenty of resources and deep-pocket connections. He could help drum up French support for the Revolution.

Washington welcomed Lafayette and assigned the French-speaking Hamilton to act as his go-between. Over time, Washington came to admire Lafayette for his courage. He relied on him for his insight. He respected him for his devotion and generosity. He regarded him as a son.

Catastrophes

The fighting season in 1777 got off to a late and bumpy start. The British occupied New York City and had an army on the move in upstate New York. Washington had his spies out, keeping track of the British troop movements led by General Burgoyne, General Howe, and General St. Leger. Intelligence came in, but Washington and his staff could not agree on what the British generals' plan of attack was going to be. This made it hard to agree on what to do in response. The Americans were still dithering when Burgoyne, in a bold and fantastic move, captured the American stronghold at Fort Ticonderoga.

The fall of Fort Ticonderoga was a strategic disaster and a psychological one, too. The fort was supposed to guard against an invasion from Canada. It also was supposed to be too tough to fail. Losing it caused a big shake-up in the Continental Army leadership as blame got passed around. Congress relieved General Schuyler of his duties in the North and put in General Gates instead.

Down at the other end of the Hudson Valley, Washington, Hamilton, and Lafayette watched what General Howe was up to and tried to second-guess his next move. Hamilton thought Burgoyne planned to head south toward Albany from Ticonderoga. He also thought this was a crazy idea without General Howe's support. Would Howe cooperate?

Congress worried that the British would storm the Hudson Valley and take over all of New York. It wanted Washington to send troops north to stop the invasion. But Washington was getting coded messages from Hercules Mulligan in New York City. Mulligan's spy network did not think the British had their sights set on New York.

Washington gambled that Mulligan was right. Congress went crazy when he sent his troops south to defend Philadelphia.

In late July, General Howe sailed out of New York Harbor with 267 ships and 18,000 Redcoats. He started north to fake everyone out, but then headed out to sea. He showed up a month later down in Chesapeake Bay.

Target: Philadelphia. No question.

Hamilton was pumped. He had been waiting months for a battle, and he felt confident. On September 11, British and American troops finally met at Brandywine Creek outside Philadelphia. The patriots put up a valiant effort but suffered a decisive and disappointing loss.

The Americans fought hard against the highly trained British troops at Brandywine Creek. They were proud of their effort even though they were forced to retreat.

A Lucky Break

The British had a chance for a complete and final victory at Brandywine Creek, but they stopped fighting to eat lunch—enough time for Washington to send in reinforcements. This is not the only example—in the Revolution or in history—when teatime flipped a British victory.

Washington soon realized that the British forces could not be stopped in their drive to Philadelphia. He sent Hamilton with a raiding party to burn the local flour mills along the Schuylkill River—it was better to destroy the mills than have them fall into British hands. The party was intercepted by a British patrol. When the British opened fire, Hamilton tried to escape by boat but was forced to swim for it.

Hamilton slogged his way to shore. He sent a hasty message to John Hancock, warning him to get the congressmen, who were still meeting in Philadelphia, out of town immediately—the British were closing in and about to attack. Meanwhile, back at headquarters, Washington received a message reporting Hamilton's death by drowning.

Both of these reports turned out to be wrong.

Hamilton showed up at Washington's headquarters shortly, much to the family's great joy and relief. And Howe put off his attack for more than a week. Congressmen forced to flee in the dead of night grumbled about being "chased like a covey of partridges," as John Adams complained. But the delay turned into a blessing. It gave the Americans a chance to gather much-needed supplies.

Washington sent Hamilton into Philadelphia to collect food, clothing, blankets, shoes, and horses—a tricky but critical assignment. Citizens did not take kindly to having their property seized, not even to keep American troops—and the American bid for liberty—alive. *Who does this guy think he is?* But Hamilton's combination of charm, tact, organization, and fairness won out. He took only what people could spare, and he provided receipts for what they gave him. He managed to send boatloads of precious supplies up the Delaware River, out of the hands of the enemy. The Redcoats who took over Philadelphia a few days later occupied a threadbare city.

Losses and Wins

Washington wasn't leaving Philadelphia quietly. He had his eye on the British troops camped at Germantown on the outskirts of the capital. He wanted to launch an attack while the troops in the city were still getting organized. The battle began in the early morning of October 4. The Americans gained the upper hand at the beginning of the attack, only to disintegrate miserably in the retreat. Even so, the outcome kept General Howe stuck in Philadelphia, unable to move. If Howe had been planning to help the British take the Hudson Valley, he could forget it now.

Poor General Burgoyne and his Redcoats found themselves in Saratoga facing General Gates's patriots without any backup. The resulting American victory was swift and spectacular. General Howe's failure to show up forced General Burgoyne to surrender his entire army of nearly 6,000 men.

With news of the British defeat in Saratoga, France joined the conflict on the side of the Americans. Up until that point, the British had been fighting a pesky bunch of musket-toting misfits whining about tea and taxes. Now they suddenly found themselves engaged in a world war with an old enemy.

The loss at Saratoga was a huge blow to General Burgoyne's ego and reputation.

The Battle of Saratoga

The war was costing the British a fortune. They needed to find a way to divide and defeat the Americans. The plan was for three generals—Burgoyne, Howe, and St. Leger—to march into the Hudson Valley from three directions. They would take over and create a blockade all the way from Montreal to New York City. This move would cut off the noisy crowd of patriots in New England from the rest of America. British forces could then team up with Loyalists in the South to end the conflict once and for all.

General Burgoyne moved south from Montreal. His troops attacked Fort Ticonderoga by hauling a cannon up the steep mountain—an extreme action the Americans did not think possible. After he took Fort Ticonderoga, Burgoyne had to take on the wilderness. He had twenty-three miles to cover but was able to move only about a mile a day. For one thing, the Americans had destroyed bridges, flooded lowlands, and chopped down trees to block the road. This forced the British to clear a new route through dense woods. For another, General Burgoyne had a ridiculous amount of stuff. He had thirty carts clattering behind him. These were filled with wine, his fancy dress uniforms, and other personal possessions. He also had 2,000 extra people—including wives, children, and servants—who followed his army's troops, along with food, bedding, supplies, and furniture.

General St. Leger—leading British troops, Loyalist militiamen, and Iroquois recruits—moved down the Mohawk Valley. Along the way, they mixed it up with local patriot militia and Iroquois who were fighting for the American side. Battles on this front eventually forced St. Leger to retreat (and sparked the start of the Iroquois civil war). He stumbled to Fort Ticonderoga, but Burgoyne had already left.

General Howe, meanwhile, was supposed to sail up the Hudson and meet St. Leger and Burgoyne in Albany. But Howe got distracted and decided to attack Philadelphia instead.

General Burgoyne ended up with no support when he got to Saratoga and suffered a stunning loss. The defeat was the turnaround America needed.

The rebel victory at Saratoga convinced the French that the Americans could win the war. France joined forces with the Americans to help crush Britain, an age-old enemy.

A Trip to Albany

News of the victory at Saratoga boosted Washington's spirits.
He set up a war council. Washington proposed shifting a hefty
portion of General Gates's troops to his thinned-out army since
New York was now reasonably secure. Washington had not been
successful in defending Philadelphia. Now he quickly needed
to fight back. The other generals agreed, and Washington sent
Hamilton to Albany to let Gates know.

General Horatio Gates

Gates and Washington had a bumpy history. In the first place,
Gates thought he should have had Washington's job and lobbied
for it almost continually. Gates questioned
Washington's leadership and second-
guessed his abilities. He puffed up his own
triumphs and criticized Washington's
defeats. Ticonderoga put Gates center
stage, and Saratoga made him a hero.
Congressmen from New England were
among his biggest fans.

In fact, history reveals that his
actual cowardice in key battles bordered
on **mutiny**, and his repeated attempts to
overthrow his commander-in-chief smacked
of treason.

Hamilton raced north at a breakneck pace to secure
reinforcements desperately needed to move the war effort
forward. In New Windsor, New York, Hamilton stopped just long
enough to inform General Putnam of the need to send his troops

south. Hamilton had the full authority to act on Washington's behalf, and his orders carried the weight of the commander-in-chief. Unfortunately, the Northern generals did not always see it that way.

In Albany, Hamilton met with General Gates. Orders were for Gates to free up brigades that were no longer needed to defend New York. Gates was offended that he had to deal with the boy wonder, and Hamilton thought Gates was a blowhard. It made for a tense discussion.

Hamilton ultimately managed to get General Gates to agree to send two brigades, though Washington hoped for three and Gates preferred to send only one. The mission was more or less accomplished.

In between meetings with General Gates, Hamilton enjoyed a break at General Schuyler's Albany mansion. While visiting, he reportedly met Schuyler's daughters, including his future wife, Eliza. He also got wind of Gates's plot to overthrow Washington as commander-in-chief. Good to know.

Philip Schuyler

Philip Schuyler (1733–1804) came from an established family with strong ties to New York and huge landholdings in the Hudson and Mohawk valleys.

As a military leader, he served as a general in Washington's Continental Army.

As a statesman, he was an elected member of the New York Assembly, a delegate to the Continental Congress, and a New York state senator. He later served in the U.S. Senate.

One of his five daughters married Alexander Hamilton.

Power and Persuasion

At a follow-up meeting, Hamilton again impressed upon General Gates the need to meet Washington's demands. Furious, Gates was forced to give in. With agreements in place and troops on the march, Hamilton saddled up to head back to Pennsylvania. Along the way, he learned that General Putnam had simply ignored his earlier order. Much-needed troops were not heading south, and the general had no intention of giving up his men. (Putnam long had it in mind to attack the Redcoats holding New York City. He was perhaps the *only* person who didn't think this was a crackpot idea.)

Hamilton took it upon himself to issue General Putnam a direct order: "I now Sir, in the most explicit terms, by his Excellency's Authority, give it as a positive Order from him, that all the Continental Troops under your Command may be Immediately marched to Kings Ferry, there to Cross the River and hasten to Reinforce the Army under him."

Washington approved of the order. But others thought Hamilton had overstepped his authority. New England congressmen who didn't like outsiders to begin with (which included New Yorkers and Virginians) picked up the smear campaign that followed Hamilton throughout his life: an impoverished, illegitimate orphan born on foreign soil is in no position to expect respect.

General Putnam did not appreciate being bossed around by Washington's young, outspoken aide-de-camp.

A Setback

Hamilton got as far as Peekskill but was taken ill and could not go on. Exhaustion and stress stopped him in his tracks. Back at headquarters, Washington received reports on Hamilton's condition. He worried as Hamilton hovered between life and death. Washington wrote: "I approve entirely all the steps you have taken and have only to wish that the exertions of those you have had to deal with had kept pace with your zeal and good intentions." Hamilton had proved himself to be indispensable. Losing him now was unthinkable.

At the end of November, Washington marched his troops to Valley Forge, eighteen miles northwest of Philadelphia. It took five more weeks for Hamilton to recover. He finally rejoined Washington on January 20, 1778—exactly a year after becoming an aide-de-camp.

Valley Forge

Life for the Continental Army at the 1777–1778 winter camp was grim. As usual, Congress proved to be the biggest threat, withholding support and supplies. But snow and disease were Washington's fiercest enemies. By spring, nearly half his men were too weak to serve or had died of disease.

The Continental Army camped out at Valley Forge for six grueling months.

When Hamilton got back to work, Washington had him write a report for Congress to describe the state of the army. Hamilton did not mince words. Troops were suffering from disease and starvation. The harsh conditions made many of them desert. They needed more supplies. Lack of support from Congress had been to blame for defeats in the battles of 1777. There needed to be more order and control. Hamilton outlined instructions and recommended reforms.

In February 1778, France officially entered the American War of Independence against Britain. As a result, the British navy had to turn its attention to fighting the French fleet on the high seas instead of supporting its troops scattered across America. British troops retreating from Philadelphia to New York City were easy pickings if the raggedy collection of patriots at Valley Forge could get it together. A big if. Washington's frozen, starving troops were on the verge of mutiny.

On February 23, Washington, Hamilton, and Lafayette greeted the arrival of Frederick William August von Steuben. Steuben was another recruit recommended by Benjamin Franklin. Steuben had been trained in the Prussian army and had ideas for improvements that were immediately put into play.

Hamilton helped translate Baron von Steuben's directions into English to create a drill manual for his boot camp at Valley Forge.

Steuben reorganized the camp to upgrade sanitation and health conditions. He set up a strict and smart training program. He drilled troop movements. He increased speed and accuracy in handling weapons. He raised the bar on cooperation and commitment. As he worked directly with one group of men, they in turn passed techniques on to others—each one teach one. The results were nothing short of miraculous. By April, Steuben had helped build up Washington's fighting force. It was now equal to whatever the British threw its way.

The Battle of Monmouth

In the searing heat of mid-June 1778, the British tried to sneak out of Philadelphia. They took their cannons, 10,000 troops, several thousand Loyalist refugees, and 1,500 wagons filled with baggage. The crush of people and supplies on the road stretched out for miles and raised a choking cloud of dust. Obviously the British were on the move. But they took a zigzag route that puzzled the Americans. Washington and his men needed to figure out where the British were going and decide what to do about it. Some of Washington's advisers favored a face-to-face conflict; others thought skirmishes and raids would be better.

General Washington, always cautious, held off his decision and bided his time. He sent Hamilton scurrying over the countryside to keep an eye on the British. Hamilton sent back a flurry of messages and reports. He alerted troops along the way to get ready. He gathered information from Washington's spies. Little by little, day by day, Hamilton convinced Washington that the British were heading for the ocean. They would make a clean getaway unless the Americans attacked.

At last Washington gave the signal, but delays and disagreements stalled everyone's progress.

Washington told Lafayette to take command of General Charles Lee's forward unit to lead the attack. Lee refused to step aside. The argument went back and forth until Washington finally gave in: Lee would lead the advance party of 5,000 men. Washington and Lafayette would command the rest.

Hamilton rode through the woods night after night to plot the exact route that the British were taking. Washington and Lafayette set out to meet up with the New Jersey militia, but Lafayette had to hold up: his troops didn't have food or water and couldn't go on in the heat.

The British had plenty of supplies. They were able to keep up their pace and had a thousand troops in the rearguard. They were not making a move to engage, but they were ready to fight back if attacked. Once they reached the coast, British warships were posted nearby. It would be a short ferry ride to safety on Staten Island.

As planned, General Lee's men attacked the British as they marched out of Monmouth. The Americans had the British outnumbered, and the rest of Washington's army was on the way. But when the British returned fire, Lee lost his nerve. He called for his troops to retreat. Lee's men who were retreating collided with Washington's men who had been ordered to advance.

Hamilton arrived to find the battlefield in chaos. He deployed troops to cover the exposed artillery. He and Washington galloped back and forth trying to reverse the retreat. Hamilton managed to avoid enemy fire, but his horse was hit. Hamilton, pinned underneath his dead horse, was pulled to safety. Badly injured in the fall, Hamilton could only watch from the sidelines as the rest of the battle unfolded.

Thanks to Washington's fierce and unfaltering courage, the troops rallied and reorganized. What might have been a loss ended in a draw. The British suffered heavy casualties but made their escape to New York City.

Washington usually kept his temper in check, but when he saw General Lee's men in retreat, he flew into a rage.

The Americans had improved skill, numbers, and opportunity on their side. They had fumbled on account of the foolish behavior and apparent incompetence of General Lee. Hamilton wasted no time in sending a report to Congress. He praised Washington's master plan and blamed General Lee for its utter failure.

Still bruised and battered, Hamilton gave stinging testimony at Lee's court-martial a couple of weeks later. Congress stripped General Lee of his command for one year.

Stuck

With the Redcoats who were fighting in the North bottled up in New York City, the British turned their attention to battlefronts in the South. Congress ordered the northern Continental Army to maintain a blockade outside New York City. And, as usual, Congress failed to offer any help to keep the fighting force going. Washington had trouble meeting even basic needs. Soldiers received Continental dollars, but inflation was so high that their pay was almost worthless. Recruiting could not keep up with separations and desertions. For the next two years, action in the North came nearly to a halt.

The Continental Congress printed paper currency but did not have the money to back it up. The British further undermined its value by putting counterfeit money into circulation. By January 1781, it took more than a hundred Continental dollars to buy a one-dollar gold or silver coin.

CHAPTER 8

Vows and Victories

We have it! We have it!

> *—Alexander Hamilton's exclamation to his men upon finally being given command at the Battle of Yorktown*

For Hamilton, who was about to turn twenty-five, the snowy winter of 1779–1780 promised to be dismal and lonely. His friend Laurens had left Washington's family with a promotion and a chance at combat in the South, something Hamilton wanted for himself. Lack of action in the North was frustrating. Hamilton was feeling unhappy and restless.

France? No Chance

Laurens was about to leave for South Carolina when Congress offered him a diplomatic position in France. He declined to take it and recommended Hamilton instead. Laurens wrote to Hamilton at the end of December to explain how the events were unfolding:

Washington moved his winter headquarters to the Ford Mansion in Morristown, New Jersey, in December 1779.

"I am sorry that you are not better known to Congress; great stress is laid upon the probity and patriotism of the person to be employed in this commission. I have given my testimony of you in this and the other equally essential points."

Nice of Laurens to say so. But in fact, delegates to the Continental Congress did know Hamilton, and plenty of them didn't like him. Some wanted their pet generals to take over Washington's command. Others didn't like being constantly baited and berated by the outspoken outsider. How could a newly arrived West Indian without ties to the heart and soil of America truly be a patriot? There was not a chance in the world that Hamilton would be considered.

But things have a funny way of working out.

Winter Games

Speaking for Washington, Hamilton regularly pestered members of Congress for supplies. Thanks to their total lack of cooperation, the storeroom at army headquarters stood empty. It was, therefore, the perfect place to set up a dance hall! It became a festive destination for everyone in town.

Hamilton's mood got a lot better with the uptick in the social scene. Fancy dress balls hosted by the officers and sleigh rides with the local daughters (a novelty for a kid from the sunny West Indies) were just the distraction Hamilton needed. He and the rest of Washington's family enjoyed the company and the parties. Presto! Chance and fortune once again combined to change Hamilton's life forever.

The Black-Eyed Beauty

Early in February 1780, Elizabeth Schuyler came to stay with her aunt and uncle in Morristown. She brought greetings from her father to Washington and to Steuben and renewed her brief acquaintance with Hamilton.

In an earlier letter to John Laurens, Hamilton had outlined what he wanted in a wife, and Elizabeth (also called Eliza or Betsey) had all the qualities he listed: She was smart, cheerful, and down to earth. She was thoughtful and loyal. She had strong feelings about faith and family. Other young men in camp admired Eliza's merry spirit, spunk, and warmth. But Hamilton, the master flirt, jumped right to the front of the line. Almost immediately, the two became inseparable. Hamilton spent every evening visiting Eliza at her aunt's house down the road from camp.

By the time Hamilton left for a meeting in Amboy, New Jersey, in early March, he and Eliza had already decided to marry. By April, he had spoken to General Schuyler and had sent Mrs. Schuyler a letter asking for her blessing. "I leave it to my conduct rather than expressions to testify the sincerity of my affection for her, the respect I have for her parents, the desire I shall always feel to justify their confidence and merit their friendship."

Eliza Schuyler and Alexander Hamilton made an immediate and unbreakable connection.

For Hamilton, whose family ties had disintegrated so long ago, Eliza's large and lively clan—three brothers and four sisters—was a bonus. And it didn't hurt that her father was one of the wealthiest and most influential men in America.

Engaged

As the fighting season got under way in 1780, Hamilton and Eliza carried out their courtship on paper instead of in person. Hamilton's letters expressed his love and longing. If he didn't hear from her for a week or so, he worried that she was having second thoughts. At one point he questioned how she really felt about becoming a "poor man's wife," cautioning her to think it through. "Your future rank in life is a perfect lottery; you may move in an exalted [sphere, or] you may move in a very humble sphere; the last is most probable; examine well your heart."

Hamilton's background may have made him feel insecure, but he didn't need to worry. Eliza wanted to be his wife with all her heart! She and her entire family adored him. We don't know how she responded, because her letters have not survived, but no doubt she was reassuring, hopeful, and loving.

Back to War

Hamilton's letters described to Eliza what was happening at the office. France's entry into the war had definitely turned the tide. Britain's resources were stretched thin, and the war with the Americans was costing a fortune. Britain could not afford to continue without some decisive victories.

Still, Britain gained some ground in battles that flared up in the South—once again thanks to General Gates. Washington prevailed on Gates to head up the campaign in South Carolina. Gates wasn't keen to take on the job and was anything but equipped to carry it out. When he blundered by positioning his troops right in the path of British forces at Camden, over 2,000 patriots were killed, injured, or taken prisoner. Gates, meanwhile, fled as the fighting broke out, putting 200 miles between himself and the men he commanded. Hamilton did not hold back in expressing his disgust.

Benedict Arnold

In America, the name *Benedict Arnold* and the word **traitor** have come to mean the same thing. But Arnold started out as a Revolutionary war hero. He stood out in battle for his bravery and skill. He played a key role in bringing down General Burgoyne at Saratoga while his commanding officer, General Gates, hid inside his tent like the coward he was. Gates took full credit for the victory and didn't even mention Arnold's name in his report to Washington and the members of Congress. Benedict Arnold was frustrated. The war was dragging on and he was overlooked for promotion. He also began to doubt that the Americans would win. So Arnold started providing the British with information about patriot weaknesses and troop movements.

The Plot

When the war picked up speed in 1780, Hamilton saw a chance to strike. Britain sent troops into the South and Hessians and Loyalists into New Jersey. This left New York without much support. Hamilton and Lafayette wanted to launch an attack on the city. Washington disagreed. He thought the troop movements in New Jersey were just a trick. Washington concluded that Britain had its eye on the forts going up the Hudson between New York City and West Point. He favored keeping West Point strong to keep Britain on its guard without putting any American troops at risk.

At the end of July, Washington offered Benedict Arnold the field command he had wanted for so long, but Arnold didn't take it. He asked to command the fort at West Point instead. Washington approved his request.

Arnold immediately started to thin the troops on duty at West Point. He sent some of them north to cut firewood. He sent some south to patrol. He assigned his gunners to escort POWs on a slow march to Tappan, New York, where Washington was based.

In September, Arnold sent a message to his British contacts. It contained plans for taking West Point and capturing the commander-in-chief, along with his top generals and his staff at the same time. He also prepared a packet of top secret documents collected at Washington's headquarters. Arnold passed the information on to the British agent John André and waited for the British attack on West Point to begin.

Back down in New York City, Hercules Mulligan and his brother were still spying on the British. They had heard that one of the top American generals was a traitor, but they didn't know which one. They also knew that supplies were being shifted around the waterfront, a sign that the British fleet was getting ready to move. They reported this to Hamilton.

Arnold had André put the papers in his boot and smuggle them to the British.

On September 25, Washington, Hamilton, and Lafayette planned to stop in the Hudson Valley to inspect West Point. They were supposed to have breakfast at the house where Arnold and his family were staying. Hamilton went ahead to say that

Washington would be delayed but to start without him. During breakfast, Arnold received a note. It said that André had been captured, and the papers hidden in his boot had been sent to General Washington. Panicked, Arnold excused himself from the table. He went upstairs and spoke to his wife and then he rushed out of the house and galloped away.

When Washington arrived a short time later, he found Hamilton with Arnold's hysterical wife. Washington glanced at the papers that had been seized from André and immediately knew that Arnold was the source. He sent Hamilton to try to catch up with Arnold, but it was too late. Arnold was already safe behind British lines. Hamilton issued orders to send reinforcements to West Point in a hurry.

Washington and his men assumed that Arnold's wife, Peggy, was completely innocent. She was mad with anguish, sobbing and screaming. She didn't even recognize Washington and could not be comforted by any of them.

It was an award-winning performance.

The men saw only the beautiful young wife with her baby, undone by her husband's evil deeds. They arranged for her to travel to Philadelphia to be with her family. In fact, she had been a main player in sending coded messages, giving up West Point, and ambushing the commander-in-chief. Working together, Mr. and Mrs. Arnold might have taken out Washington, Hamilton, and Lafayette before lunch.

If Peggy Arnold had kept quiet, her role might never have been revealed. But on her way to Philadelphia she stopped to visit her friend Theodosia Prevost and told her the whole story. Theodosia was the wife of a British officer, but her lover (and future husband) was an American officer named Aaron Burr. Theodosia shared Peggy's secret with him.

News of Benedict Arnold's treachery spread, fanning the fire of freedom. Americans who were tired of the hardship after years of war renewed their commitment to the cause.

Eliza's Friend, John André

The British spy caught smuggling Benedict Arnold's papers was the handsome and gallant Major John André. André was a poet, artist, and musician. He was widely admired by both British and Americans for his charm, polish, refinement, and elegance. By coincidence, he had spent time under house arrest at the Schuylers' mansion. All of the Schuylers liked him, especially Eliza.

Hamilton admired André, too, and may have tried to save him. The British commander received an anonymous message suggesting a prisoner swap between André and Benedict Arnold. The commander refused, assuming Hamilton was behind the request and knowing that the Americans would immediately put Arnold to death if they got their hands on him.

Hamilton changed tactics. If he couldn't save André, he could at least get Washington to show some mercy. Hamilton argued that simply carrying papers didn't automatically make André a spy. If André had been acting as a messenger, he could be executed by firing squad—the sentence for a gentleman—instead of going to the gallows as a criminal. Washington didn't buy it. He needed to make an example of André, and the review board agreed.

In the end, André placed the noose around his own neck and used his handkerchief as a blindfold.

Disappointments

Hamilton might have hoped that the leadership he showed in the Arnold–André plot would finally get him a field command since they were now down a general, but Washington didn't share that notion. In October, Lafayette was getting ready to make a move on Staten Island and suggested that Hamilton lead a battalion. Washington refused. He needed Hamilton's counsel, language skills, swift pen, and sound judgment now more than ever. When Hamilton asked to lead a raid in northern Manhattan, he reminded the general that he really wanted to be a soldier, not a clerk. Washington canceled the mission. Over the next several weeks, Washington withheld an overdue promotion, balked on a recommendation for an advisory position, and blocked diplomatic missions to France and to Russia. Hamilton postponed his wedding so Washington wouldn't be short-staffed when less critical staffers went on leave for weddings of their own. As the tedium went on and on and Hamilton's resentment and frustration mounted, the only saving grace was Eliza. "I am in very good health and shall be in very good spirits when I meet my Betsey."

Changes

At last the end of November rolled in. The army headed for its winter camp, stopping what little fighting there might have been. Hamilton and a friend rode north, and on December 14, 1780, Alexander Hamilton married Elizabeth Schuyler.

After a few weeks off to relax, consider his future, and enjoy the Schuyler hospitality, Hamilton reluctantly returned to work. He rented a cottage near the winter headquarters in New Windsor, and Eliza joined him there.

Troop mutinies, British victories, and a staffing shortage did not give Hamilton a chance to raise the possibility of being given a field command. The tense and touchy Washington was in no mood to consider it.

On February 16, 1781, Hamilton and Washington had a misunderstanding. Hamilton could have waited for Washington's bad temper to pass and then could have offered the general an apology. But he didn't. Instead, he quit his job as aide-de-camp.

Hamilton's Side

Hamilton wrote to his father-in-law to explain the rift. The general had asked to see Hamilton, who said he'd be right there and then went downstairs to deliver a message and speak briefly to Lafayette.

"Instead of finding the General as usual in his room, I met him at the head of the stairs, where accosting me in a very angry tone, 'Col Hamilton (said he), you have kept me waiting at the head of the stairs these ten minutes. I must tell you Sir you treat me with disrespect.' I replied without petulancy, but with decision 'I am not conscious of it Sir, but since you have thought it necessary to tell me so we part.'"

When Washington later cooled down, he reached out and asked Hamilton to meet with him. Hamilton declined. He had had it. Hamilton agreed not to broadcast the falling-out and to stay on until a French-speaking aide-de-camp could replace him. Meanwhile, he once again got passed over for a command and watched Lafayette deploy to Virginia instead of him. In May, Hamilton left Washington's family for good.

Hamilton went back to Albany and took time to study and write and talk to Eliza and her older sister, the lively, witty, intelligent, and beautiful Angelica. But he couldn't stay away for long. He knew that the last campaign of the war was coming, and it would be decisive. He did not want to miss out on the action.

General Schuyler wanted Hamilton to remain in Albany to become a delegate to Congress. Lafayette wanted him in Virginia to command his artillery. Hamilton wanted what he had always wanted—a chance for glory. He went back down to New Windsor and got a room near headquarters so he could continue his writing and keep up with what was going on. At the same time, Hamilton never stopped pestering Washington for a chance to lead in combat. At one point, he even went so far as to threaten to resign from the army altogether.

On July 31, 1781, Washington finally agreed to give Hamilton the field command he had always wanted. He was twenty-six years old.

Yorktown

Washington was considering an attack on New York City when, on August 14, word came that a French fleet was heading for Chesapeake Bay. It would be available only until the middle of October. When hurricane season was over, it had to head back to the West Indies. At the same time, Lafayette reported that the British were setting up camp in Virginia. If Washington wanted to take advantage of the situation, he needed to act quickly.

Washington sent a letter that made it look like he was still getting ready to attack New York City. Hamilton sent a letter to Eliza to say that nothing much was going on. Washington and Hamilton meant for British spies to pick up both messages, which they did. The letters helped hide the fact that the true target was Virginia. Secrecy was key.

Hamilton got his troops shoes and supplies for the overland journey. Every day, he had his men up and going well before dawn. They moved quickly, through forests and fields, past villages and towns, across creeks and rivers. They headed for the Chesapeake, where the French fleet would be waiting.

On September 9, Hamilton would have been stopped cold if he hadn't gotten a loan from the French commander to pay his troops. They had marched 200 miles and weren't going any farther. Cash persuaded them to continue. They boarded open boats for the journey across the bay. The dangerous crossing took a week. The French fleet fought off the British out in the Atlantic to keep the rebels safe. At last the troops came ashore at Williamsburg. Hamilton joyfully reunited with Lafayette and Laurens for the push to Yorktown.

The French fleet took on the British in the Battle of the Virginia Capes while the Americans crossed the Chesapeake.

The Lay of the Land

Redcoats commanded by General Cornwallis had set up camp in Yorktown to provide a deepwater harbor for the British fleet. Water surrounded Yorktown on three sides, and attacking the town by land was not easy to do. An open plain, a marsh, and two creeks blocked the way. Cornwallis fortified the site. He built batteries of artillery connected by trenches. The trenches were guarded by ten small forts, called *redoubts*. The redoubts were protected by moats filled with a tangle of sharpened stakes.

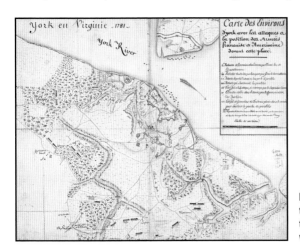

If the British couldn't hold their line in Yorktown, their only way to escape would be by ship.

Preparations

When the Americans and French got to Yorktown, the French engineering corps started digging the first of two side-by-side trenches to establish their line. The trenches would get the troops closer to the British line and keep General Cornwallis contained. When Cornwallis realized what the American and French were up to, he nervously called for backup. He was told the British fleet would be on its way from New York on October 5.

In Your Face

Military tradition called for a celebration when trench work was complete. Hamilton and his men hopped down into the first trench with drums pounding and flags flying. The British responded with a volley of cannon fire. The British then watched in amazement as Hamilton led his troops out of the trench and onto the field to go through a series of marching drills. The British were apparently too shocked to fire a shot. Other officers criticized Hamilton's risky move even though the men were safely out of range. Caught up in the moment, Hamilton just couldn't resist showing off with this grandstanding display as the British watched.

On October 9, Washington lit the first fuse to start the siege. Cannon fire blasted day and night with deadly force. By October 11, the news for General Cornwallis and his Redcoats was bad: the Americans had knocked out most of the British guns, and the British reinforcements were still stuck in New York.

Washington setting off the first cannon at the Battle of Yorktown.

The Americans started work on the second trench to move the line forward. Progress was blocked by redoubts nine and ten. They needed to be taken out.

Time to strike. Washington ordered the French light infantry to attack redoubt number nine, while Lafayette and the Continental Army attacked number ten.

Hamilton's Shot

Lafayette tapped his aide to lead the charge, but Hamilton begged Washington one more time to let him take command. He pointed out that he had seniority and was the officer of the day. Washington agreed.

Finally!

Hamilton was triumphant and more than ready for action.

On the night of October 14, cannon fire lit up the night, signaling the start of the raid. Hamilton and his 400 men leaped out of the trenches and ran across the quarter-mile stretch of open ground under enemy fire. On orders from Washington, their guns were unloaded and their bayonets fixed to move silently, but their war whoop split the sky. They covered the distance so fast that they caught up to the rebels clearing the sharpened stakes out of their way. Hamilton didn't break stride. He used the shoulder of a kneeling soldier to vault over the parapet, swinging his sword and urging his men to follow.

Hamilton and his men used surprise and skill to carry out the raid with extraordinary bravery and speed. The din and clamor of hand-to-hand combat filled the night. It took only ten minutes to capture the fort.

When the fighting stopped, Alexander Hamilton had become exactly what he always wanted to be—a war hero.

Hamilton, leading the attack, was the first man to reach redoubt ten.

The End

Control of redoubts nine and ten meant that the Americans and the French could move up their artillery and pound away at the British front at close range. Early in the morning of October 16, the British attacked the French troops holding the center of the line but only briefly interrupted the cannon fire. Late that same night, in a final effort, General Cornwallis tried to escape across the Yorktown River. When a storm swirled up, his boats capsized. The British were finished. There would be no retaliation and no retreat.

On October 17, a British soldier appeared on the barricade beside a drummer boy. He was waving a white handkerchief to signal a ceasefire.

On October 18, the generals and their aides met and agreed on the terms of surrender.

The next morning, American troops and French troops faced each other in two mile-long lines marking a path out of Yorktown. General Cornwallis's defeated Redcoats marched between them. When they reached the open field, the British laid down their arms.

Within a week, Alexander was on his way home to Eliza in Albany.

As Cornwallis and his men surrendered, the British fleet finally left New York carrying 5,000 troops to help defend Yorktown. Too little, too late.

CHAPTER 9

Lawyer and Delegate

We have now happily concluded the great work of independence, but much remains to be done to reach the fruits of it.

—A letter to John Jay, July 25, 1783

I t took a long time for the war to wind down. Battles continued to flare up. Hamilton's dearest friend, John Laurens, was killed in a South Carolina raid on August 27, 1782, almost a year after Yorktown. The British occupied New York City until 1783. Peace talks began in Paris in April 1782, but it took months to communicate back and forth across the ocean. The final treaty was not ratified until early in 1784.

Life in Albany

Leaving the army gave Hamilton a chance to settle down. But that didn't mean that he slowed down. He was now twenty-seven. He felt he needed to make up for the years gobbled up by the war. He snagged a chance to fast-forward a law degree. Studying law would be the quickest way to jump from soldier to statesman. He could build on the power base he already had— friends in high places—and support his family, too. He relied on the reputation of his father-in-law, but he did not want to rely on his money.

First-born Son

Philip Hamilton arrived January 22, 1782—the first of eight children born to Alexander and Elizabeth Schuyler Hamilton. Hamilton cherished his children and cared for them with love and concern.

Hamilton moved his family from the Schuyler estate to a little house in Albany. He gave one friend a room in exchange for tutoring. He borrowed office space from another. He and Aaron Burr, another fast-track student, shared law books from several places, including Philip Schuyler's extensive law library.

Hamilton had to learn scads of information in a short amount of time. A handbook of laws and rules would have been a helpful study guide. Such a guide didn't exist, so Hamilton used his notes to create one. As he studied and paced, he read his own book aloud.

For eager young American lawyers like Hamilton, there would be plenty of work to do—New York banned Tory lawyers from appearing in state courts.

In July 1782, Hamilton passed the bar. He had been in a hurry to become an attorney, but he wasn't in a hurry to set up a practice while the British were still in New York. Instead, he turned his attention to politics.

Aaron Burr

As soldiers and students, Hamilton and Aaron Burr crossed paths many times. It is easy to see how they might have become rivals. New York City was not very big.

Aaron Burr came from a background of education and privilege. Like Hamilton, he had been orphaned at an early age. He finished college before the war started and joined the army in 1775. He was known for his heroic courage in the northern campaigns. As the rebels fled New York City, he helped lead them out of harm's way (through the forest that is now the Upper West Side).

Burr's good looks, popularity with the ladies, and quick intelligence matched Hamilton's, but his personality was very different. Burr was serious, quiet, and guarded. He and Washington did not get along; at about the time Hamilton joined Washington's family, Burr left it. He ended up serving as General Putnam's aide-de-camp.

After the war, Hamilton and Burr ran in the same circles. They both moved their young families to Wall Street. They both practiced law and often met in the courtroom. They both were involved in building the new nation.

Ideas and Insights

Hamilton's studies helped him keep shaping his ideas about government. Hamilton thought that big-ticket items like trade laws could not be subject to the whims and interests of individual states. America needed a strong center, which the Articles of Confederation failed to provide.

At the top of Hamilton's list was setting up a way for the new nation to collect money (like from taxes and tariffs) and then spend it (like to support the Continental Army). Part of the reason the war had dragged on for years and years was because Congress didn't have any way to raise the money to pay for it. Hamilton had had plenty of experience dealing with this weak and powerless system.

An Example

When the messenger showed up in Philadelphia to tell Congress about the victory at Yorktown, Congress couldn't pay him. Congressmen passed a hat, and each of them put in a dollar.

The Americans were independent, but they were flat broke. Hamilton thought this big problem needed to be solved. To do it, states would have to agree to support the common good.

In the spring of 1782, Hamilton had been appointed to be the state tax collector of New York. It was a thankless job, but it added fuel to Hamilton's funding fire. All of the states had huge bills to pay, both to the soldiers who fought the war and to the foreign nations that pitched in. Citizens going back to their pre-war lives were just glad the whole thing was finally over. Many of them assumed that paying taxes was voluntary.

For one thing, Congress was kind of a joke. People did not recognize what had proved to be such a weak and flimsy governing body. Instead, they supported their state and local officials. Once the Treaty of Paris was signed, many felt that Congress could just disband: it wasn't needed anymore. Besides that, the British still occupied most of New York, jamming up progress and blocking the main ports. Even Hamilton would have a hard time getting anyone to budge while the British were still around.

The T Words

Taxes and tariffs were still very sore subjects. *Remember the Stamp Act? Remember the Boston Tea Party? If you think we are going to pay taxes and fees to bring goods in and out of port, think again.* No one wanted to pay into a common fund. No one wanted to discuss a set of trade laws that would be applied to all citizens across all the states.

At the end of July, New Yorkers appointed Hamilton to represent them at the Confederation Congress. Here was his chance to bring his concerns and his solutions to the table. He could see that trying to collect money to pay debts put the cart before the horse. First you needed to set up a government and give it the power to oversee issues that applied to everyone. Then you could set up the tax and trade laws under the central authority.

Almost everyone in Congress had agreed to overthrow Britain. But few congressmen agreed on what American independence would look like after the war was over. Some assumed that everyone could just go on about their pre-war business. The independent states would each be a country— like the countries of Europe. A committee meeting could be held once in a while to check in. Others—like Hamilton— wanted to form a single nation, with a strong government to unite all the states under one leader and one set of laws.

In November, Hamilton went to Philadelphia for his first term in Congress. From the moment the session began, it was tough going for a guy who had the bigger picture and longer view in mind.

Give and Take

In January 1783, high-ranking army officers led by Alexander McDougall came to address Congress. The army was at the end of its rope. Soldiers worried that once the peace treaty was signed and the British left New York, the army would disband. They would never get the money they were owed. Officers presented Congress with a warning: "The uneasiness of the soldiers, for want of pay, is great and dangerous; any further experiments on their patience may have fatal effects." The message was clear: pay up, or get ready to fight a civil war.

Hamilton and several other members of Congress hatched a plan to exploit the threat of mutiny without letting it happen. To pull off this plan, they needed help. Hamilton turned to a man he could trust, and trust to get the job done: George Washington. Hamilton reconnected with Washington and let him know how bad the financial situation had become. He asked Washington to step in with his influence and leadership. "Your Excellency should preserve the confidence of the army without losing that of the people. This will enable you in case of extremity to guide the torrent, and bring order perhaps even good, out of confusion." In effect, Hamilton and the congressmen used Washington and the Army to force Congress to act. They urged troops to start laying the groundwork for an armed action.

Washington agreed with the officers' demands but not with their methods. He called an officers' meeting and told them that they should not do anything to "lessen the dignity and sully the glory" of their victory. He told them to trust Congress to do the right thing. He started to read his prepared statement, then apologized for having to stop and pull out his glasses. "I have not only grown gray but almost blind in the service of my country."

The men immediately backed down out of respect for their commander. They owed it to Washington's sacrifice and leadership. A vote to support and cooperate with Congress was unanimous.

Hamilton helped pull together a plan to pay the soldiers back wages, provide pensions, and help widows and orphans. Congress, glad to avoid a mutiny, quickly agreed to it. Of course, there wasn't any money to honor this plan. Congress still needed to agree on a way to get it.

Hamilton saw his chance. He proposed lumping all the states' IOUs for their troops into a national debt. That way everyone could quit squabbling over what was fair and whose share was whose. Tax collectors would work directly for Congress. But this kind of central power was exactly what worried those who wanted each state to have its own control.

Just like that, Hamilton lit the fuse to set up a **federal** government.

Washington knew what was at stake as he addressed the angry officers. But he believed that keeping the peace was more important than using military force.

Treaty of Paris, 1783

Congress told the Americans attending the peace talks in Paris to keep the French in the loop at all times. Terms of any agreement with Britain had to square with America's allies. But France and Spain had agreements of their own, which brought Spain to the table, too. It got complicated.

By chance, on August 3, 1782, John Jay ended up at that table speaking for the Americans by himself. Thomas Jefferson's wife had recently died, so Jefferson was sailing home. Henry Laurens (John's father) was a POW being held in the Tower of London. John Adams was busy wheeling and dealing with bankers in Amsterdam. Benjamin Franklin was feeling under the weather.

The Spanish representative pointed at the map. He proposed drawing a line from Lake Erie to the Gulf—roughly from Detroit down through Columbus, Atlanta, and Tallahassee on today's map. Everything east of the line would belong to the United States; everything west of the line would belong to Spain.

Jay looked at the line created by the Mississippi River, about 400 miles farther west, and had a different idea.

Jay left the meeting. He went and woke up Franklin. France—and Spain—had to be left out of the peace talks no matter what Congress said. Jay knew that if they were included, France and Spain would end up claiming a lot of territory. Team USA needed to get a bigger piece of the continental pie.

In the final draft, the Mississippi marked the western border of the United States. This made the land area of the United States bigger than any country in Europe. The resources were unlimited. Trade partners were eager to do business. Thanks to Jay, the treaty not only gave the Americans their independence: it also gave them their very own empire to go with it.

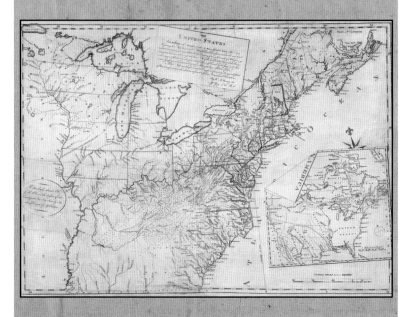

CHAPTER 10

The Power of the Pen

I fear that we shall let slip the golden opportunity of rescuing the American empire from disunion, anarchy and misery.

> —Letter to George Washington during the Constitutional Convention, July 3, 1787

In the fall of 1783, Hamilton moved his family to a house on Wall Street in Manhattan, a few doors down from the Burr family. On November 25, Evacuation Day, the Redcoats marched out of town for good. They left the city in a mess. They had never made repairs after the fire at the beginning of the war, and they simply let things fall apart.

Loyalists Go Home!

Patriots who had fought the British resented their fellow citizens who had lined up with the enemy. They wanted Loyalists' property seized and their rights restricted, even if their families had been in America for generations.

Loyalists streamed out of the city. Some set sail for England. Some crossed the border into Canada. Those who stayed were bullied and browbeaten. Everyone was suspicious of anyone who had ever had dealings with Tories. Even Hercules Mulligan did not escape mistrust. He would have been run right out of town if Washington hadn't been seen eating breakfast with him after the Evacuation Day ceremony.

Evacuation Day was a joyful occasion, marking the end of the war after years of sacrifice. But peace presented many obstacles to overcome and difficulties to face. Independence was not going to be easy.

Hamilton was horrified. For one thing, he thought the Americans should show some understanding. They could not build themselves up on a foundation of anger and bitterness. The war was fought for freedom. That had to apply to friends and enemies alike. You didn't have to agree, but you had to get along.

More important, Hamilton saw the exit of Loyalists as a drain on the economy. The United States was losing merchants with strong ties to trade partners and goods. It was losing artisans and skilled laborers. It was foolish and shortsighted to let this source of income flow out to sea.

Most of all, Hamilton believed in upholding the law. Regardless of what side anyone had been on during the war, everyone was subject to the same laws and regulations now. It was unjust to treat Tories as outcasts bound by a different set of rules. The Loyalists had a right to equal protection.

Hamilton would soon become one of the top lawyers in New York City. He counted many Loyalists among his clients. He spoke out against laws passed by New York that violated the terms of the international treaty. It was another way for Hamilton to push for a federal government that would unite the states as a single nation. For Hamilton, a strong central government was the only option.

Get It Together

The states struggled along in the postwar world. Some of them had money, some of them didn't. Pairs of states argued over borders and trade agreements. Some states imposed taxes, some didn't. Some states that had plenty of money were not making any payments to cover the war debt. Every state had its own best interests at heart. Civil unrest was running high; cooperation was mostly nonexistent.

Overseas, allies were losing faith with the American states. States couldn't pay back their debts, and no one in Europe was willing to extend them any credit. If America couldn't borrow funds to rebuild, the country was going to sink. What's more, even a whiff of a fracture between one state and another could give any foreign power a chance to sweep in and take advantage of the situation.

In September 1786, Hamilton was part of the New York delegation to attend trade talks in Annapolis, Maryland. Something had to be done to fix what was so clearly broken. Maybe by focusing only on the trade questions, progress could be made.

Only twelve delegates from five states even bothered to show up. On the plus side, the smaller group could actually reach an agreement about something: the Articles of Confederation needed to be overhauled.

After months of delay, a raft of rebellions, and further collapse of the fragile framework holding the states together, the Constitutional Convention was scheduled to meet in Philadelphia the second week of May, 1787.

The Constitutional Convention

The Constitutional Convention finally got under way at the Pennsylvania State House on May 25. It had been eleven years since the Declaration had been signed in that same place. Everyone had put in so much time and effort to gain their freedom. Having that dedication in common was a good starting place.

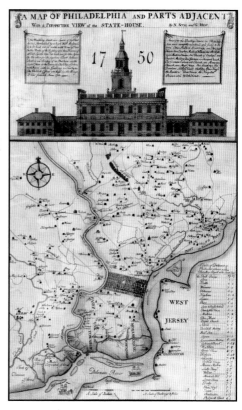

Fifty-five delegates arrived for the meeting. Every state except Rhode Island sent a representative. Hamilton was surrounded by plenty of people who opposed a federal government, but there were supporters and friends on board, too. He had reason to feel hopeful, and he was eager to get started.

The Pennsylvania State House was later renamed Independence Hall.

The Rules of Convention

Hamilton was on a committee to set up the rules the delegates would follow:

* There would be complete secrecy. Nothing that was said or discussed would leave the hall. Each delegate needed to be able to speak freely without a chance for gossip—no leaked information, no leaked misinformation.

* Washington was put in charge of the proceedings.

* Delegates were given writing paper, quills, ink, and resources. History and philosophy books and pamphlets were provided for the men to use while they worked.

* Delegates would stand and face Washington to speak, and everyone would pay attention. No one could interrupt a speaker. No one could be reading while someone had the floor.

* Everyone would stand respectfully at the end of the day and allow Washington to leave the hall first.

From the opening gavel, one thing was clear: this would not be a meeting to revise the Articles of Confederation. Most of the delegates agreed that that document had served its purpose. Now it needed to be replaced by a stronger, more specific, and sturdier document that would meet the needs of the future.

With uncharacteristic restraint, Hamilton let the other delegates have the floor. He listened intently to their ideas, concerns, and solutions. He quietly bided his time, fine-tuning and organizing his thoughts.

Delegates from Virginia proposed a fifteen-point plan. It supported a two-house Congress. The people would elect their representatives to the first house. That body would appoint representatives for the second house from a list of nominees provided by the state government. The Congress would then choose an executive. The number of representatives would depend on population.

The delegation debated the pros and cons of each of Virginia's points. Big states liked Virginia's ideas, small states didn't. Hamilton saw the battle lines being drawn. How would federal and state governments be coordinated? And how would smaller states have the same clout as the larger states?

Hamilton understood why the small states were upset. The delegations from larger states could run right over them. And Hamilton actually had lots of misgivings about what he felt

Hamilton had spent years imagining the perfect government. His plan combined the sturdy, ongoing foundation of a monarchy with the freedom of a republic.

were the dicey parts of democracy. Elections left up to citizens reminded him too much of mob rule. He wasn't sure every ordinary citizen was up to the task. But the discussion continued. Hamilton still did not weigh in with his own proposals or concerns. Not yet.

Hamilton Cuts Loose

Finally, on June 18, after waiting nearly three weeks, Hamilton stood up and faced George Washington. He cleared his throat and started speaking.

Hamilton proceeded to outline his plan for the new nation:

- The people in each state would vote on a board of electors. The electors would then vote for proposed candidates.

- The legislature would have two houses. The assembly would serve three-year terms. The senators would serve for life.

- The legislature would appoint courts for each state.

- The legislature would maintain the national army and navy—states would not have their own militias.

- State laws could not contradict federal laws.

- An executive would be voted on by the electors and would serve for life.

- The executive would command the military.

- The executive could veto legislation.

- Judges would serve for life.

Hamilton praised what he felt were the smart parts of the British parliamentary system. He proposed an executive branch that sounded a lot like the British **monarchy**. The delegates sitting silent must have squirmed in their seats—not only because Hamilton expressed some ideas that made them want to jump up screaming their objections, but also because he just would not stop.

Hamilton spoke for six hours straight!

When he finally sat down, his fellow framers sat speechless. The meeting adjourned for the day.

Some of Hamilton's points match the form of the federal government we have today. He was in favor of three branches of government: executive, legislative, and judicial. The legislative branch would have two houses (the Assembly, which corresponds to today's House of Representatives, and the Senate). The executive would command the national military.

But much of his plan was over the top. And it was too close to the British system. His own delegation from New York, for example, would never, ever go for it. Over the next few days, Hamilton spoke up to address one point or another. As time went on, however, he was not feeling optimistic. The long, slow parade of motions and discussions and reports from a dozen different committees made progress seem impossible. Dejected, Hamilton went back to New York to attend to some business. He promised Washington he'd return soon "if I have reason to believe that my attendance at Philadelphia will not be mere waste of time."

Hamilton, the Monarchist

Hamilton's enemies at the Convention took note of how closely his plan matched the British system of government. Hadn't he attended King's College and protected the Tory college president from the mob? Hadn't he associated with Hercules Mulligan, who was known to cater to Redcoats and Loyalists? Hadn't he defended John André, a British spy whose aim was to hand over West Point and murder George Washington in cold blood? Wasn't he speaking out for Loyalists' rights in the courts of New York? And now this. Appointments for life? This was nothing short of a monarchy, pure and simple. Some even said Hamilton intended to bring King George III's son to America to rule. Many were happy to silence the West Indian brat. They never stopped raising his supposed British sympathies to make him look bad. These accusations dogged Hamilton's steps for the rest of his life.

Conversation and Compromise

The Convention continued for three more months. Right about when Hamilton returned to Philadelphia, the other delegates from New York left. They were not willing to give up any of New York's power to strengthen a federal system. Not a particle.

Meanwhile, the framers hammered out their differences point by point. They finally agreed to a two-part legislature. Each state would get the same number of senators, but the number of representatives would depend on the state's population.

Northern and southern states disagreed loud and long over the question of slavery, though their concern was in regard to ownership, not inhumane treatment of other people. Slavery was an issue in every state. Coming to some agreement about it was a must. The whole idea of founding the nation depended on figuring this out.

As representation based on population looked certain, slave states wanted enslaved people to be included in the count. Smaller states in the North called foul. The compromise was to count each enslaved person as three-fifths of a person and deny enslaved men the right to vote.

Hamilton was uncomfortable with this so-called solution, but he could see that everything would collapse without this agreement. It was unjust, but it was necessary.

Hamilton and Slavery

Hamilton's experiences as a child in the West Indies made him an outspoken opponent of slavery his whole life.

During the Revolution, Hamilton and his friend Laurens lobbied to recruit enslaved men, promising them freedom in exchange for their service in the army. Hamilton reasoned—correctly—that if Washington's army didn't offer freedom to these men, Britain would. Both Hamilton and Laurens saw the hypocrisy of fighting for their own freedom while holding others captive. Their effort to form a battalion of freed men was unsuccessful, though thousands of freed men did indeed fight on both sides of the Revolution.

In 1785, Hamilton helped found the New-York Society for Promoting the Manumission of Slaves. The society helped raise money to buy enslaved people's freedom. He was among those who petitioned the New York legislature in 1786 to end the slave trade, "a commerce so repugnant to humanity, and so inconsistent with the liberality and justice which should distinguish a free and enlightened people."

Hamilton believed that the government needed a rock-solid center to balance the shaky unpredictability of democracy. But he also could see that most of the measures the framers could agree to accept were much better than nothing. He was glad to get three branches of government with checks and balances onto the list. He was able to give up having the president and senators serve for life. He was okay with providing a way for states to propose amendments to the Constitution. By September, the Committee of Detail submitted the first draft of what would become the Constitution. Hamilton, as part of the Committee of Style, started revising each point to put it into a proper format.

The Committee of Style presented the final draft of the Constitution to George Washington.

THE PREAMBLE

Members of the Committee of Style were William Johnson of Connecticut, Rufus King of Massachusetts, Gouverneur Morris of Pennsylvania, James Madison of Virginia, and Alexander Hamilton of New York. Gouverneur Morris wrote the preamble to the Constitution:

> *We the People of the United States, in Order to form a more perfect Union, establish Justice, insure domestic Tranquility, provide for the common defence, promote the general Welfare, and secure the Blessings of Liberty to ourselves and our Posterity, do ordain and establish this Constitution for the United States of America.*

The Preamble is followed by seven Articles.

The Signing

On September 17, 1787, thirty-nine of the fifty-five Convention delegates signed the Constitution. Of those who didn't sign, the New York delegates (apart from Hamilton) rejected the entire document on principle. Some non-signers objected to the idea of the Electoral College. Some wanted the document to include a Bill of Rights. Some thought the states gave up too much power.

The Hard Sell

The Convention sent a copy of the Constitution to the Confederation Congress at the end of September 1787, and Congress sent it on to the states. At least nine states had to **ratify** the Constitution before it could go into effect. Articles criticizing the document began to appear almost immediately in the press.

Now the real struggle began. Now was not the time to withdraw from the game. Hamilton shook off his own personal opinions. Whatever Hamilton failed to achieve at the table in Philadelphia, he more than made up for in his zeal to see the Constitution ratified.

Hamilton enlisted the help of fellow framers John Jay and James Madison. They needed to publish a series of essays to defend and promote ratification. Hamilton was about to write his way into history, using the full measure of his talent.

James Madison was a shy, bookish Virginian with a quiet manner and a first-class mind. Hamilton enlisted Madison's help because he was an expert on political history.

The men planned to write twenty-five essays using the pen name Publius. (They ended up writing eighty-five.) The essays were published between October 1787 and August 1788 in the New York press. A two-volume collection of the essays called *The Federalist* was published in 1788.

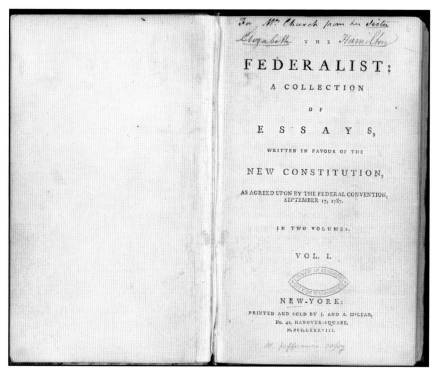

According to the inscriptions, Eliza Hamilton gave this copy of *The Federalist* to her sister Angelica Schuyler Church. It wound up in Thomas Jefferson's library, and Angelica may have passed it on to him herself—they became friends during his time in Paris.

Authorship of *The Federalist* was kept secret, but historians have been able to assign essays to each writer. John Jay wrote four before he became ill and only wrote one more later on. Madison wrote twenty-nine of the essays. Hamilton wrote fifty-one.

The essays set out to explain the Constitution, point by point. The watershed of words that Publius pumped out on the fly—up to three essays in a week—made it hard for anyone else to get a word in edgewise, either to question or to object.

Word Count

The Constitution, establishing a new government = less than 5,000 words.

The Federalist essays, explaining the Constitution = about 190,000 words.

While Hamilton churned out essays, he also prepared to do verbal battle in New York State. As part of the rules committee for the Constitutional Convention, Hamilton had slipped in a provision. It directed state conventions to debate every Article before voting to ratify. This gave him an advantage on his home turf. No one could argue the Constitution's details as knowledgeably—or as long—as Hamilton could.

By the time the New York convention came around, eight states had ratified already. Hamilton could talk long enough to be convincing. He could talk long enough to wear out the opposition. And he could talk long enough to stall the proceedings until that ninth state—either New Hampshire or Virginia—put the Constitution over the top. Win-win.

The Federalist No. 15

Why has government been instituted at all? Because the passions of men will not conform to the dictates of reason and justice, without constraint.

—Published in The Independent Journal, December 1, 1787

Celebrate!

On July 23, some 5,000 merchants, artisans, and craftsmen held a parade in New York City—a celebration for the new Constitution. Bakers displayed a loaf of bread that was ten feet long. Brewers pulled a 300-gallon keg of ale on a cart. Coopers hauled barrels made with thirteen staves, one for each state. Sailmakers waved a flag with Hamilton's face painted on it, honoring the local guy who had fought so hard for everyone, both on and off the field. A float shaped like a ship sailed down Broadway, pulled by a team of horses. It was christened the Federal Ship *Hamilton*. A cart that followed carried a billowing banner:

Behold the federal ship of fame

The Hamilton we call her name;

To every craft she gives employ;

Sure cartmen have their share of joy.

Cannons fired, and people cheered.

That Manhattan morning was Hamilton's moment in the sun. A moment, but not much more.

By the time New York ratified the Constitution on July 26, 1788, the new government was already established. New Hampshire had the honor of being the ninth and deciding state, ratifying on June 21. Rhode Island didn't sign on for nearly two more years.

The "more perfect Union" was under way.

CHAPTER 11

A Member of the Cabinet

. . . the most enlightened friends of good government are those, whose expectations are the highest.

—*from* The Report on Public Credit, *January 9, 1790*

N o one but George Washington could lead the new nation. No one wanted the job less. Hamilton had urged Washington to accept the challenge. Washington responded, "It is my great and sole desire to live and die, in peace and retirement, on my own farm."

Hamilton wouldn't take no for an answer. Success depended on Washington. Anyone else might bungle the job, and failure would spell disaster. Washington was key to uniting the states into the United States. Hamilton appealed to Washington's sense of duty.

Washington's Election

Right out of the gate, Hamilton had problems with how the leadership was chosen. He could not imagine jump-starting the new nation with anyone but Washington in charge. Washington would rule fairly. He would compromise thoughtfully. He would smooth feathers that were already starting to ruffle.

Prior to the election, Hamilton felt stressed about whether John Adams could beat Washington and what would happen if he did. And Governor George Clinton of New York had his hat in the ring, too. He hated everything about forming a federal government, didn't like Hamilton, and was one of Philip Schuyler's biggest rivals.

Unthinkable.

Hamilton felt compelled to steer votes away from Clinton. But what if they went to Adams instead of Washington?

Unthinkable!

Hamilton need not have worried. Washington was the unanimous choice of the Electoral College.

But Hamilton did worry, and it made him try to pull strings behind the scenes to influence the outcome. In a foolish move, he urged the electors from Connecticut, New Jersey, and Pennsylvania to swing their votes.

The government was barely underway, and already Hamilton distrusted the system he'd played a huge part in crafting. His motives may have been pure, but that didn't make it okay. John Adams took it personally when he got wind of it, which of course he did. Hamilton did not necessarily intend to humiliate the sensitive grump from Massachusetts, but nonetheless he had.

Hamilton was brilliant. But that didn't stop him from using bad judgment, acting on impulse, making hasty choices, and showing lack of control.

George Washington understood these failings that so often got Hamilton into trouble. He was forgiving. Others were not, and many of them were keeping score.

On February 4, 1789, electors from ten states made Washington the first chief executive of the United States.

Prior to 1804, each elector cast two votes for president. The candidate with the most votes became the president; the runner-up became vice president. George Washington was named on every ballot, making his election unanimous. John Adams received the second-highest number of votes, so he became the vice president.

A national celebration welcomed Washington to New York for his inauguration on April 30.

Washington was fifty-seven years old when he took the oath of office as the first president of the United States.

When Hamilton married Eliza, he gained an enemy in Governor George Clinton of New York. Not only did Clinton have a long-running feud with Philip Schuyler, he also supported the interests of New York State at the expense of the United States.

Once Washington became president, Hamilton went after Clinton. Clinton was running for re-election in the 1789 New York governor's race. Hamilton was bent on crippling Clinton's political career once and for all. He used his pen and the press to launch a full-throttle attack on Clinton's character.

Voters were not persuaded and Clinton was re-elected. Bad feelings lingered on both sides.

In a crafty surprise move, Governor Clinton offered the office of attorney general to Aaron Burr. Burr accepted. Hamilton saw this as a stab in the back. Burr had spoken out against Clinton in the race! But Burr liked power as much as the next guy—if not a tiny bit more. He saw the offer as an opportunity.

What's in a Name?

Congress met for the first time on April 1. The House of Representatives met on the ground floor of the Federal Hall in an open gallery. The Senate met upstairs in a closed chamber, no guests. (The Senate's "secret sessions" continued for five years.) The agenda in both chambers was miles long, but the first order of business was deciding titles of address, which promised to be a very touchy subject.

From the beginning, George Washington knew that the office of chief executive had to be presented as being worthy of respect without being regal. Those who thought the Federalists were monarchists at heart were on the lookout. The title couldn't be anything that sounded noble or overblown. Adams, as president of the Senate, suggested that Washington be called "His Highness, the President of the United States and Protector of their Liberties." Noble *and* overblown!

The anti-monarchist patrol had a field day. *Adams is planning to be crowned king for sure! He must be raising his sons to be princes!*

Compare and Contrast

At his swearing-in ceremony, Washington wore a plain brown suit made of cloth woven in America—setting a buy-local example. It was his habit to take a walk every afternoon. Adams moved into a fancy mansion overlooking the Hudson. He pranced around New York City in a gaudy carriage and powdered wig, enjoying plenty of glitz and glamour.

The House of Representatives pared Adams's idea down to "President of the United States," and the Senate agreed. Some referred to the stout vice president as "His Rotundity." Washington asked people meeting with him in person to call him Mr. President.

A set of rules and customs for the new president to follow did not exist. Washington realized that everything he did would set the tone for the new nation, and he wanted to get it right. He tried to strike a balance between keeping his distance from the public as leader and acting like an ordinary citizen.

Getting Started

Members of the executive branch of the brand new government faced some challenges for the first and only time in the history of the United States. Elected officials coming later could build on successes, pinpoint failures, and avoid pitfalls. This first group did not have that luxury. They cobbled together their experience and their knowhow and blazed a bumpy path into the future.

Right away, Representative Elias Boudinot of New Jersey— the man who had befriended Hamilton when he first came to America—floated the idea of setting up a Finance Department. The outcry and outrage were instantaneous. Lawmakers trotted out the same objections that had always been so quick to boil over. Any solution to the financial crisis brought up a laundry list of unpopular topics. And a treasury secretary, acting with the power of the president, could start poking his nose into everybody's business. Been there.

Even so, everyone had to admit that the new nation's finances were a mess, and nothing could be accomplished if the government didn't have any money. Also been there. Besides that, Washington couldn't serve all alone in the executive office. Clearly, having the Constitution in his hand and his thinking cap on his head wouldn't be enough to lead the nation. He needed help. He needed input, instruction, and insight from advisers. He needed to set up his cabinet.

The Cabinet

The cabinet system of government comes straight across the Atlantic from Great Britain—which may be why the Founding Fathers didn't specifically call it that when they wrote the Constitution, though in Article II, Section 2 they refer to "the principal Officer in each of the executive Departments." The origin of the term comes from a small room where private meetings are held.

Today there are fifteen cabinet departments. Washington started out with three: Hamilton was secretary of the treasury, Jefferson was secretary of state, and Henry Knox was secretary of war.

On September 2, 1789, Washington created the Treasury Department. On September 11, he nominated Alexander Hamilton to be the treasury secretary of the United States. Hamilton was thirty-four years old.

The Senate confirmed Hamilton's appointment that afternoon.

The Obvious Choice

Hamilton came with high praise and glowing recommendations from the other men whom Washington had considered to head up the treasury. Everyone who knew Hamilton knew about his interest in economics. During the war, his friends had teased him for lugging around giant books about economic theory and history. He had devoted hours to designing the perfect financial system, defining the building blocks and fixing the stumbling blocks. He had a fair idea of the extent of the nation's debt and good ideas for stopping the downward spiral. It would take cooperation and patience. People would have to be willing to make some compromises and take some risks. These conditions posed huge problems for lawmakers, but Hamilton was confident it would work.

Hamilton also knew he was the obvious choice for treasury secretary. Did he have misgivings or mixed feelings? Maybe.

For one thing, taking the job meant taking a whopping pay cut. Hamilton had a growing law practice and a growing

family—he and Eliza now had four children. He was in demand as a lawyer and was paid well for his services. Working for the government and making ends meet would not be easy.

Hamilton was the best person— maybe the only person—who could solve the huge national debt problem and get the United States moving in the right direction.

For another, Hamilton had already worked with Washington for years. He knew all about Washington's moods and bad temper and relentless demands. On the other hand, Washington needed him—a man he could trust. And who would pass up the chance to make this kind of mark on history? Not Hamilton.

Hit the Ground Running

The treasury secretary's responsibilities fell neatly into Hamilton's wheelhouse. In some ways, he had been training for this position his entire life. He hired a staff and got to work.

Part of the job was simply housekeeping—money in, money out. Hamilton's mother had taught him to keep exact and detailed records when he worked in her shop, and he studied double-entry accounting in college. He quickly and efficiently set up methods for bookkeeping, checking, and auditing.

Taking charge of customs also felt like familiar territory, thanks to Hamilton's first job with Cruger. This was a big part of the treasury secretary's job because it was a main source of much-needed revenue. Hamilton immediately contacted customs collectors in each state to report on traffic, shipments, and payments. He wanted to see cargo lists. He needed to know what goods were coming and going and how much there was.

When the reports came in, Hamilton could see right away that they were off. From his days working the docks in St. Croix, he knew about the culture of smuggling, graft, and bribery in the shipping business. He also knew about maritime law from his own caseload in his law practice. Hamilton requested a fleet of ten cutters to enforce the trade laws. Patrols would discourage **privateers** who were costing the United States precious revenue.

He also suggested to Washington that each boat be built in a different shipyard and that the sails be made in the United States.

Congress believed—and Hamilton agreed—that anything that improved trade helped the nation. It charged the Treasury Department with enforcing the Lighthouse Act. As the first lighthouse superintendent, Hamilton put together a list of lighthouses, beacons, buoys, and piers up and down the coast. He oversaw the construction of a lighthouse in Chesapeake Bay. He calculated how much whale oil lighthouse keepers would need to keep the lanterns lit and added the cost to his budget.

Watery Legacy

Hamilton's Revenue Marine later became the U.S. Coast Guard. The Cape Hatteras Lighthouse, dedicated in 1803, was known as Mr. Hamilton's Light.

The Elephant in the Room

The main issue that Hamilton had to address was the war debt. It was huge and getting bigger as interest mounted. Hamilton submitted a repayment plan in a report to Congress on January 14, 1790. The plan made sense. It recommended adding the war debt of each state to the existing federal debt to create one giant amount. The debt would be easier to manage and would let all the states make a fresh start. Hamilton also recommended a tax on luxury goods. This would include wines and spirits made in the United States, along with coffee and tea. He reasoned that people who could afford luxuries could afford to pay a little extra for them.

Reaction to the report was mixed.

Some people understood finance and agreed with Hamilton's reasoning. They appreciated the elegance and genius of his plan.

Some understood finance but didn't like Hamilton. They attacked his character but hopped quickly into the marketplace, hoping for a windfall by investing in Hamilton's solutions.

Some didn't understand finance. They suspected Hamilton of trying to pull a fast one.

Some didn't understand finance and didn't like Hamilton. They accused Hamilton of trying to pull a fast one.

Extreme Reactions

Hamilton expected James Madison, his friend and co-writer of *The Federalist*, to help back him up. But reactions started to fracture along North-South lines. Madison took sides against Hamilton with the planters of Virginia. Most of the war debt was carried by the Northern states. Some of the Southern states claimed to have already paid off what they owed. They didn't think they should have to pay more. Or again.

As Congress argued about Hamilton's plan, lawmakers from the South disagreed more and more strongly with lawmakers from the North. The fight highlighted old grievances, simmering suspicions, and deep divisions. Like packs of wolves, big-city swindlers would fleece the hardworking lambs toiling in the rural farms and fields. Wealthy merchants should pay their share of the debt instead of lining their pockets. Never mind that the wealth of the Southern plantation owners was built on the backs of enslaved Africans—a fact that many may have been thinking but no one discussed. Congress had already tabled legislation calling for an end to the slave trade and an end to slavery altogether. Arguments on the House floor grew bitter and angry. But Southerners were wary. Anything that made the executive branch stronger—including voting in favor of Hamilton's plan—was a threat to the institution of slavery.

According to the House rules, Hamilton was not allowed to present the report himself. (The British system allowed members of the executive branch to sit in on the legislature; the Americans were having none of it.) Hamilton might have been able to use his clever way with words to argue and clarify—and influence and sway. He instead had to sit silent in the gallery and watch as his ideas got presented and then shredded. Miscommunication turned into mistrust as one speaker shouted down another.

Hamilton had spent years fine-tuning every detail to create a successful and sustainable economy. When he at last had the chance to put his ideas into action, the United States House of Representatives all but shut him down.

And it was hard for Hamilton not to take it personally when people said nasty things about him. Hamilton had always been thin-skinned when it came to criticism. Blasting his ideas was bad; badmouthing his character was even worse. He felt frustrated and miserable.

Location and Relocation

Part of Hamilton's proposal passed in June. The question of states' debts got sidelined as Congress turned its attention to another hot-button issue. Article I of the Constitution called for a federal district—a neutral territory of not more than ten square miles to be set aside as the seat of government. It did not specify where this place would be.

Arguments about the location of the capital mirrored the debt disagreement—rural farmers against urban merchants, South against North. Behind the scenes, lots of haggling was going on. Northerners wanted the capital to stay in New York. Members from the South didn't like that idea. They pushed for a swampy stretch along the Potomac.

Hamilton wanted the capital to stay in New York, but he was willing to use it as a bargaining chip. In return for his funding plan, he would promise his opponents in Pennsylvania and New Jersey support for a federal district in Germantown or Trenton. This tactic mostly fizzled. Pennsylvania and Virginia may already have had a deal in place: Philadelphia would be the temporary site and the Potomac would be the permanent site. Pennsylvanians assumed that the move from a temporary to a permanent location would stall over time. Wishful thinking.

Congress Hall in Philadelphia

The Dinner-Table Bargain

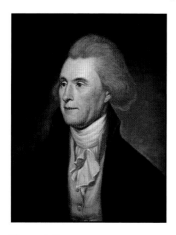

Thomas Jefferson, secretary of state

Jefferson liked discussing matters over dinner with small numbers of people. He invited Madison and Hamilton to dinner in mid-June, and they resolved both the debt problem and the capital problem.

According to Jefferson's account, he could see that it would be in everyone's best interest to get things settled and move on. (It is likely that Jefferson had already urged Southern lawmakers to get on board with Hamilton's plan, but he didn't tell that to Hamilton.) Jefferson didn't agree with having states' debts added to the federal debt, but the bill had to pass, and the sooner the better. The Union depended on it. And in Jefferson's role as secretary of state, stronger credit overseas was a must.

On the flip side, promising that the federal district would move to the Potomac would ease tension between Hamilton and the leadership in the Southern states. And think how many people would benefit: Madison had already bought up tracts of land nearby in Virginia. Washington lived just down the river, and Jefferson lived just down the road. Everyone would be happy.

Hamilton was not known for his ability to find common ground, especially with Jefferson. But somewhere between the main course and dessert, he agreed to support the Potomac site. In return, the members of Congress from the South who were blocking his debt plan would vote to approve it.

This cartoon shows Congress sailing on the "Constitution of America." The ship is sailing for Connogochegue (current-day Washington, D.C.) by way of Philadelphia.

Ties that Bind

For Hamilton, moving the site of the capital in return for getting his debt plan approved was an easy call. He would have preferred to see the capital stay in New York City to create a strong political and financial center modeled after Paris or London. But there were sixteen cities lobbying to host the new federal district, and Hamilton didn't have strong ties to any of them. He was a newcomer and an outsider. For him, the United States was his home but not his homeland. Jefferson, on the other hand, had deep connections to his Virginia birthplace, where his family had farmed for generations. The closer Jefferson could be to his beloved Virginia, the better. For him, the site on the Potomac was the only choice.

By August, Congress had passed Hamilton's plan to pool the federal and states' debts, and the seeds were planted to create the city of Washington in a federal district called the Territory of Columbia.

CHAPTER 12

Decisions and Disgrace

Alas, alas, how weak is human nature.

—Abigail Adams in a letter to her son, Thomas, describing Hamilton

I n September 1790, the Hamiltons and the seat of government moved from New York to Philadelphia. The city of Philadelphia was well stocked, thanks to exotic trade routes and a lively marketplace. It was also well organized, with paved streets and street sweepers.

"And why can we not have an American bank?"

Hamilton set up his office—a pine desk, a couple of planks on sawhorses, and a growing staff—and got right back to work. In planning and pulling off economic wonders, he kept on thinking big. His economic structure was in place. Now he needed a national bank. The country needed a national bank! It would bulk up business and issue one form of currency for everyone to use.

Hamilton had been considering the bank's

Hamilton's ideas about banking and the future of the United States were visionary. He set up the system that allowed private enterprise to grow and prosper.

establishment for over a decade. News that a bank might be in the works got huge support from Dutch investors. They offered the United States a million dollars and the same credit rate given to other nations. Even so, many lawmakers who were hearing about it for the first time did not warm to the idea.

A Change Change

The framers of the Constitution understood the need to set up a uniform monetary system that made financial sense. They also knew that Americans did not trust paper money; they had watched the value of Continental dollars dwindle down to nothing. Coins minted under the authority of the federal government would replace the jumble of things that passed for currency at the time: colonial and foreign money, livestock, farm products, and moonshine.

This Turban Head Gold $5 Half Eagle is one of the first gold coins minted in the United States.

Jefferson promoted using the decimal system with the dollar as the unit of currency. And both Hamilton and Jefferson agreed that making coins beautiful and thick with ridged (reeded) edges would make them harder to copy and harder to clip. (Coin clippers could carefully trim the edges of smooth coins. They sold the shavings and still could spend the clipped coins at face value.) Hamilton wrote the report and pushed a bill through Congress to set up the U.S. Mint. He was disappointed when Washington made it part of the Department of State.

Some who opposed forming a bank believed the institution to be evil at its core. Nothing would convince them otherwise. Jefferson went so far as to suggest that anyone who worked for a bank was committing treason and should be put to death.

Some worried about the increasing and over-reaching size of the federal government—what Thomas Jefferson called "the invasions of the legislature." They doubted that the bank was constitutional. Lack of understanding made others suspect the complicated scope of Hamilton's ideas.

The bank bill passed. But the opposition—led by Madison and Jefferson—urged Washington to use his veto power to shut it down. Hamilton—in a 40-page argument—used the Constitution to defend the bill. He described the implied powers and defined the meaning of "necessary and proper." Hamilton's report gave the Constitution flexibility and power. It didn't just describe a system of government. It provided a guide for governing.

Split Decision

When Washington signed the bill to establish the bank, he still wasn't sure it was constitutional. But the people who weighed in against it didn't convince him otherwise. Washington might have flipped a coin. Instead, Washington's policy when the cabinet didn't agree was to side with the department directly involved. Otherwise he would have had to ask for Hamilton's resignation. Game, set, match for Hamilton.

In the decades since, lawmakers and judges have upheld Hamilton's broad interpretation of what is "necessary and proper," citing his arguments and acknowledging his brilliance.

Setting up the Bank of the United States left a trail of resentment and ill will. It caused a wider split within the cabinet itself. It made a deeper rift between North and South. It gave some people stronger misgivings about the federal government. It convinced others that Hamilton had a hidden agenda.

You'd think that Hamilton would have been on his best behavior to mend fences, improve his standing with his critics, and rebuild connections in the cabinet and in Congress. You'd be wrong.

Going Corporate

Hamilton's next pet project focused on his vision for America as a world leader in manufacturing. Hamilton's amazing foresight imagined the coming of the industrial age. He knew the U.S. would be left behind if it didn't start turning its resources into goods. To cut down on competition, import duties could be raised on products Americans made for themselves and lowered on raw materials. Starting with his banking system, Hamilton laid the groundwork for setting up corporations.

Hamilton put his mind to figuring out how to sneak blueprints for machinery out of Europe and encourage skilled factory workers to emigrate. He planned to build a workforce that included women and children instead of slave labor. He wanted to coax foreign investors to funnel money into U.S. enterprises.

Hamilton's vision of America horrified Thomas Jefferson. To him, Hamilton's plans presented a deadly threat to life in the rolling countryside of farmland and pasture.

Jefferson believed that banking and bond trading were get-rich-quick schemes. They made fortunes for a small number of people. Money gambled on investments would be better spent supporting the common good. Hamilton's plans to build corporate America would create an elite class of wealthy businessmen that rivaled the power of the Tories—exactly what the patriots fought against in the Revolution. Jefferson pulled farther and farther away from the Federalists and their supposed ties to Britain. He set the stage for creating a new political party.

Mistakes and Missteps

Hamilton's behavior when it came to beautiful women had long made him a lightning rod for gossip. He might have guarded his reputation and made sure that no one had anything to discuss. But instead, he used his boyish charm to flirt his way through socials and dinner parties. He made almost no secret of his strong attraction to Eliza's favorite sister, Angelica, whenever she visited. One summer, he put her up in a nearby townhouse while Eliza and the children stayed at the Schuylers' in Albany. (Senator Schuyler finally told Angelica to rejoin her family in Europe.) These behaviors were well known to Hamilton's critics and made him a target for con artists.

On a July evening in 1791, while he sat working on his master manufacturing plan, Hamilton was interrupted by a young woman named Maria Reynolds. She asked to speak to him in private and tearfully told him that her husband had deserted her. She turned to Hamilton as a fellow New Yorker, hoping he would help her get back home.

Hamilton went to Maria's house that evening with the cash she needed to pay her fare. He should have gone right back home again, but instead he stayed. What might have been a business arrangement turned into an affair. Hamilton could have ended the relationship without any lasting consequences, but he didn't.

Within a few weeks, Maria's husband showed up to confront Hamilton. James Reynolds demanded money and threatened to tell Eliza. Hamilton made the blackmail payments. But he also kept seeing Maria off and on for over a year.

Hamilton finally cut his ties to Maria and stopped responding to her husband's demands in August 1792—when he and Eliza welcomed their fifth child. But James Reynolds had connections and a big mouth, so plenty of insiders got wind that something was amiss.

Risky Business

Some historians suggest that Hamilton felt sorry for Maria because her husband treated her badly, a situation that perhaps reminded him of his mother and her first husband. Plus it is possible—and even likely—that Maria and her husband worked together from the start to set Hamilton up in order to blackmail him. The fact remains that Hamilton freely and knowingly made a lot of bad choices with regard to Maria Reynolds. He and his family eventually paid very dearly for his mistakes.

Troubles Brew

James and Maria Reynolds were just the start of Hamilton's problems. In March, one of Hamilton's top aides went spectacularly and completely broke in a scheme that involved a large sum of money "borrowed" from the treasury. The news caused a panic among investors in New York and nearly collapsed the Bank of the United States. In spite of Jefferson's efforts to prevent Hamilton from taking action, Hamilton pushed for a government bailout and narrowly avoided disaster.

Madison and Jefferson tried to have Hamilton fired, and they called on Congress to investigate wrongdoing. Hamilton was cleared; but in the process, anti-Federalists gained strength. As the dust from this scandal settled, Madison and Jefferson's Democratic-Republicans (what came to be today's Democratic Party) stood in fierce opposition to Washington and Hamilton's Federalists.

Yet another problem stemmed from disagreements about France, which added to the tension between Jefferson and Hamilton. Jefferson had spent years in the French court. He felt that the United States needed to pay its war debt to France even though the French king had been executed during the French Revolution. Hamilton argued that the United States didn't have an agreement with the French Republic. Its agreement had been with the French king. No king, no IOU.

Hamilton thought that Britain was an important trade partner. Britain supplied the United States with everyday goods that everyone needed. Partnering with Britain's global trade network made good economic sense. Hamilton was making deals with British shipping while Jefferson as secretary of state was pushing for closer ties to France.

Jefferson blamed Hamilton's attitude on his love

Hamilton was feeling the strain of his career and his personal life. Political opponents who did not want to risk criticizing the beloved George Washington hammered away at Hamilton instead.

of anything British over anything French. Jefferson once again accused Hamilton of secretly being a monarchist. Tempers flared in cabinet meetings and spilled over into Federal Hall.

Washington actually agreed with Jefferson about repaying the debt to France. But he also agreed with Hamilton that now would be a bad time to turn the presidency over to someone else. The growing conflict between the Federalists in the North and the Democratic-Republicans in the South put the future of America on thin ice. For the sake of the fragile Union, Washington would run for re-election.

And remember James Reynolds? Still a problem. At the end of November, Reynolds and a partner were arrested for trying to embezzle money from the government. When Hamilton refused to get the charges dropped, Reynolds's partner tipped off Speaker of the House Frederick Muhlenberg. Reynolds supposedly had information that would bring Hamilton down. Muhlenberg passed this unsettling claim on to Senator James Monroe and Congressman Abraham Bedford Venable, both Virginians and both Democratic-Republicans.

The three questioned James Reynolds. Reynolds accused Hamilton of using treasury funds to speculate for his own gain. When Maria Reynolds was questioned, she backed up her husband's story.

What to do? The Congressmen could have taken the information straight to President Washington, but they decided to run it by Hamilton first. On December 15, the three showed up at Hamilton's office. Aaron Burr came with them, acting as Maria Reynolds's lawyer. When confronted with the charges, Hamilton denied everything. He could explain!

At a meeting that evening, Hamilton assured the congressmen that his dealings with James Reynolds had nothing to do with anything about the Treasury Department. He showed them proof in the form of love letters from Maria. He gave them way too many details about their relationship. The congressmen agreed to drop the whole thing. It was a private matter, nothing to do with them.

But James Monroe picked up the packet of Maria's love letters on his way out. He passed them on to Jefferson for safekeeping. Jefferson liked to collect information. The letters might come in handy later.

Backbiting and Backtracking

Throughout the first part of 1792, Hamilton deflected a battery of accusations leveled by Jefferson through his stooges in Congress. Hamilton may have been foolish at times and reckless at others, but his recordkeeping was exacting and exemplary.

Everyone should have been relieved that Hamilton was honest. If he had wanted to steal from the treasury, siphon off foreign loans, or hide a shortfall—all claims made against him—he could easily have embedded the information

James Monroe and his fellow Virginians, Jefferson and Madison, worked to block Hamilton in any way they could every time they got the chance.

where no one would have ever found it. Instead Hamilton answered the charges. He buried Congress in hundreds of pages that documented his every move as treasury secretary. The investigations were long and tiresome for everyone. They also were a total waste of time. Madison voted against Hamilton every chance he got, but he was one of the few.

In spite of Jefferson's best efforts, Congress upheld Hamilton's claim that he had never used any public money for his own private gain. But this did not mean that the attacks on Hamilton's character would stop.

Washington and Adams won re-election. Washington hoped that Jefferson and Hamilton would knock off the infighting during his second term. But they continued to wrangle right up until Jefferson resigned in September. Hamilton planned to resign, too, but his decision was derailed. An outbreak of yellow fever sent everyone fleeing from Philadelphia, and government came to a halt. Hamilton and Eliza both got sick and went to Albany to recover. Hamilton could have gone from Albany back to New York to pick up his law practice and his former life, but right then the Whiskey Rebellion heated up.

The Whiskey Rebellion

In 1791, Congress had passed a tax on spirits distilled in the United States. Farmers in western Pennsylvania howled, taking their cues from Jefferson to voice their objections. The tax favored the wealthy merchants in the North and stuck it to the poor farmers. Growers turned their crops into liquor to make it easier to transport, store, and sell. Some of them could pass the tax on to the buyers, but for many in that part of the U.S., money was scarce. Farmers buying liquor couldn't afford the price hike. Farmers using liquor as currency couldn't sort out the red tape. Everyone in the region refused to pay the tax.

Washington tried to keep the peace and urged the farmers to comply with the law. But by 1794, resistance to the tax had escalated and tempers ran high. Local farmers marched on Pittsburgh. They burned down the tax collector's house and threatened to torch the entire city before moving on to the seat of government in Philadelphia.

Washington was nervous about where the uprising would lead, and rightfully so; sympathizers on both sides vowed to take a stand. In the new nation, it was impossible to predict whether the Union could withstand the crisis. Hamilton advised Washington to send a militia to quell the rebellion. Together, Washington and Hamilton led 13,000 troops into Pennsylvania. It was a convincing show of force. By the time the soldiers reached Pittsburgh, only a few farmers lingered. The two rabble-rousers found guilty of treason were pardoned by President Washington. President Jefferson repealed the tax in 1802.

At last, Hamilton told Washington he was ready to leave the treasury. That didn't mean he planned to leave the government. He was the Federalist Party leader. It was only natural that he would consider higher office. As George Washington prepared to step aside, Hamilton's star began to rise. Briefly. Maria's letters had been circulated. As soon as supporters mentioned Hamilton's name as a possible presidential candidate, his enemies threatened to expose the affair.

On January 31, 1795, Hamilton left the job of secretary of the treasury and left Philadelphia. He wrote Angelica to tell her of his resignation. "Having contributed to place those of the Nation on a good footing, I go to take a little care of my own; which need my care not a little."

CHAPTER 13

A Matter of Honor

Every day proves to me more and more that this American world was not made for me.

— *Letter to Gouverneur Morris, February 29, 1802*

H amilton began his retirement from public life by joining his family on an extended getaway at the Schuyler mansion in Albany. He spent the spring traveling and relaxing. He put ads in the Manhattan papers to get back his law books that had been borrowed by friends and colleagues. He set up his Manhattan office. He needed money to support his still-growing family— baby number six was on the way—and by summer his law practice was up and running again in Manhattan.

Time with his family in Albany gave Hamilton a chance to relax and plan his next move. Some thought he would run for governor of New York, and others thought he had his eye on the presidency. Was he really finished with public life?

Suspicion and Humiliation

While Hamilton practiced law, his work with George Washington might have been out of sight, but it was not out of mind. Washington continued to call on Hamilton to share concerns, offer opinions, and write speeches, including the seventh State of the Union report to Congress and his farewell address.

At the same time, Hamilton was still being called upon by Congress to defend his actions during his time as treasury secretary. The Democratic-Republican press hounded him in articles and editorials. Once again the name James Reynolds bubbled to the surface. Hamilton was accused of stealing from the treasury and paying off Reynolds to keep him quiet about it.

Hamilton had always been ultra-sensitive about his honor, something that was well known, so it was easy for his enemies to push his buttons. Too easy. Congress had investigated Hamilton's department and upheld his reputation several times over. The congressmen who had confronted him about Maria Reynolds five years earlier knew that Hamilton's dealings with James Reynolds had nothing to do with treasury, even though they were slow to say so now. The Democratic-Republicans were playing Hamilton. They must have been shocked—as many, many people were—by Hamilton's response.

Instead of ignoring his critics, who knew there was no truth to the charges, Hamilton decided he needed

It was important for Hamilton to clear his name. He offered an apology and defended himself against false charges.

to launch a defense. He had to clear his name and protect his financial system. In August 1797, he published a full account, describing in painful detail his affair with Maria Reynolds and her husband's blackmail. Hamilton admitted being guilty of breaking his marriage vows. He had betrayed Eliza and brought shame upon himself and his family, but he wasn't a thief.

The Reynolds Pamphlet, as the confession came to be known, caused an uproar. Henry Knox commented: "Myself and most of his other friends conceive this confession humiliating in the extreme." The Democratic-Republicans rejoiced as Hamilton's standing in the political arena hit a major speed bump. So did President Adams.

John Adams came from a modest family but could trace his Massachusetts roots back for four generations. He believed that Hamilton could not appreciate American patriotism because he was born in the West Indies. As for the Reynolds affair, what would you expect from someone with Hamilton's background?

Major General Hamilton

Hamilton regained some ground midway through 1798. The war brewing between France and the rest of Europe had spilled over into the West Indies, putting U.S. trade ships at risk. The Federalist hawks wanted President Adams to get tough with France. Adams took the opportunity to build up U.S. military forces. He asked George Washington, now retired, to come back on board to command the army. Washington agreed, but only if Hamilton was named second in command. Hamilton got a promotion and was appointed inspector general.

Hamilton was honored to be given the rank of major general but had issues with Congress, as Federalists and Democratic-Republicans argued over what action to take against France. Still, he managed to help set up the U.S. Navy and use it to pummel the French fleet in the Caribbean, and he drafted a plan to set up a U.S. military academy.

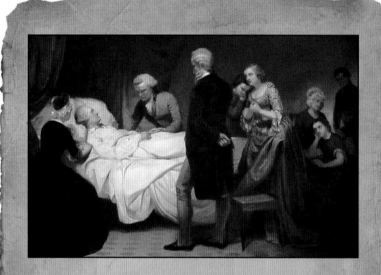

The Death of George Washington

George Washington went out riding on a stormy day and didn't change out of his wet clothes until after dinner. He developed a sore throat that soon turned into an infection. He died on December 14, 1799.

Hamilton's life would not be the same without his trusted friend and loyal defender. He wrote to Martha Washington: "No one, better than myself, knows the greatness of your loss."

When Washington died at the end of 1799, Hamilton expected to head up the army in his place. But there was no love lost between Adams and Hamilton. Adams never thought of Hamilton as anything but a despised foreigner. In Adams's mind, Hamilton was no better than a gatecrasher, especially considering who his parents were. Adams negotiated peace with France—no need for an army, no need for a commander. He was glad to disband the military altogether rather than give Hamilton the command.

Bitter Defeat

In the messy election of 1800, factions, self-interests, regions, and competing ideas were all in play. Hamilton went after Adams, who was running for re-election, but his main goal was to defeat his hated rival, Jefferson. And Aaron Burr was on the ballot too. As far as Hamilton was concerned, all three of them were bad choices.

In trying to tip the scales of power, Northern Federalists pledged to vote for Southern Federalists, and Northern Democratic-Republicans pledged to vote for Southern Democratic-Republicans. But would they? Hamilton backed Charles Cotesworth Pinckney of South Carolina. He was banking on the Federalist vote from the North and hoping at the same time to split the Southern vote away from Jefferson.

Epic fail.

Adams and Pinckney both lost, and the Federalist Party disintegrated completely. To make things more complicated, the two Democratic-Republicans, Jefferson and Burr, tied for first. Since a tick in the Constitution stated that the two top vote-getters would be elected president and vice president, the presidency was now up for grabs. (The Twelfth Amendment fixed this issue to make the president and vice president a separate vote.) The House of Representatives would decide.

As much as Hamilton hated Jefferson, he at least believed him to have a moral compass. Burr, not so much. Hamilton urged the Federalists in the House to withhold their votes rather than support Burr. "Tis not to a Chapter of Accidents, that we ought to trust the Government peace and happiness of our Country. Tis enough for us to know that Mr. Burr is one of the most unprincipled men in the UStates in order to determine us to decline being responsible for the precarious issues of his calculations of Interest."

On November 17, 1800, Congress held its first session in Washington, D.C.

The new Capitol Building in Washington, D.C.

On February 11, 1801, the House of Representatives held its first ballot. Sixteen states got to vote, so a majority of nine votes was needed to win. The House balloted thirty-five more times before a decision was reached. On February 17, Thomas Jefferson became the third president of the United States. Aaron Burr became vice president.

Once Jefferson and Burr were elected, Hamilton's political life faded.

An Affair of Honor

Hamilton could argue for pages and days over details and differences. When disagreements got personal, he had a very short fuse. His sorry start in life put a chip on his shoulder. Over the years, Hamilton had tangled plenty of times with anyone who questioned his honor. In the custom of the day, a personal insult could lead to a duel. A challenge could be resolved without bloodshed, but it could not be ignored without losing face.

Hamilton's sensitive streak rubbed off on his firstborn son, Philip. And so it was that when George Eacker badmouthed the Federalists in general and Major General Hamilton in particular, Philip wouldn't leave it alone. A shouting match between Philip and Eacker followed several months later, and the challenge was made.

In many cases, an **affair of honor**, as dueling was called, could be carried out mostly for show, especially in the North.

So-called "single combat" in the Southern states was serious business. In the North, it was discouraged, and in most states it was illegal. Showing up was often enough to settle differences with honor. Shooting to kill was not the desired outcome, and most wounds were not life-threatening.

Dueling Rules

Duels followed a strict set of formal rules. Twenty-six commands make up the Irish *Code Duello*, written in 1777. Affairs of honor in the United States followed these guidelines. Here are the basics:

* Once the challenge is made, the person who starts the quarrel apologizes. If the apology is accepted, that is that. The matter is settled. This first step can take a while. Letters are exchanged. Grievances are aired.

* If the apology is not accepted, then each opponent asks a friend to stand in. This friend is called a *second*. The seconds try to settle the quarrel to everyone's satisfaction. If they can get the parties to apologize, the problem is solved. If they can't reach an understanding, the seconds set the time and place for a duel.

* The person challenged chooses the weapons and the place.

* The challenger chooses the distance.

* The seconds decide on the time and terms of the firing. The firing can be by signal or by command.

Throwing away your first shot, called a *delope*, was a way to satisfy your honor without hurting anybody. It gave your opponent a chance to return a harmless shot rather than commit cold-blooded murder. Most duels did not prove fatal to either party.

On November 23, Philip Hamilton and his second rowed across the Hudson to New Jersey to confront George Eacker. It has been reported that Philip's uncle and his father both advised him to throw away his shot.

At first neither opponent fired when the second yelled, "Present!" Eacker finally shot first; Philip's shot missed as he fell.

Philip died the following day with his helpless parents by his side. To compound the tragedy, the shock of Philip's death caused his seventeen-year-old sister, Angelica, to suffer a complete mental breakdown. She lived into her seventies but never recovered.

Philip Hamilton

The New-York Evening Post

On November 16, 1801, Hamilton and a group of like-minded Federalists published the first issue of the *New-York Evening Post*. Running his own newspaper gave Hamilton a platform. He was able to use it to express his views about Jefferson and to wage his battle against slavery, among other things. The editorial board didn't hide its Federalist background (and backers), but it vowed to present interesting and honest information without regard to party.

In a sad twist of fate, one of the paper's first news stories reported the death of Philip Hamilton on November 24 at age nineteen.

NEW-YORK EVENING POST.

Retreat

Hamilton's private grief showed in his public presence. Subdued sorrow replaced the sharp edge and energy that had marked his career. He watched Jefferson settle into a low-key, unflappable administration. Thanks to Hamilton's vision, the economy hummed along in a nation that enjoyed peace and prosperity. But Hamilton felt depressed and defeated. He could not understand the easy appeal of the Democratic-Republicans. And he worried about the need to strengthen "the frail and worthless fabric" of the U.S. Constitution. He expected it to snag on the slightest crisis and unravel completely.

Hamilton kept up his writing and his law practice, but he spent more time with his family at their home in Harlem, nine miles north of the city. Hamilton was glad to walk the grounds and stroll in the woods. Eliza was glad to have everyone under one roof. For years, the family had been split by Hamilton's duties. Week in and week out, he had taken the older kids, and she kept the little ones. In the summer of 1802, when their new house was finished, the Hamiltons' eighth child was born, and everyone was together.

Hamilton named his house the Grange after his father's family mansion in Scotland and his uncle's plantation in St. Croix. The property overlooked the Hudson and Harlem rivers and included fifteen acres of gardens, an orchard, outbuildings, and woods.

Old Wounds

In the spring of 1804, Vice President Aaron Burr was on the outs with President Jefferson. He wouldn't be asked to join the ticket for a second term. Burr was looking for his next job, so he threw his hat into the New York governor's race. In the course of the campaign, Burr had a gripe with one of the newspaper publishers, and the press went after him. Story after story ripped his character and misrepresented his record. He pretended it didn't bother him, but Burr's touchy personality took a hit. When he lost the race by a big and embarrassing margin, he looked for someone to blame. He picked Hamilton.

Hamilton and Burr had been sniping at each other off and on for nearly thirty years as they competed for the same goals: glory, fame, power. On the verge of being sidelined for good, Burr decided it was time to speak up for himself. On June 18, 1804, he had his second, William Van Ness, deliver a letter to Hamilton's office. The letter called out Hamilton for every nasty crack he had ever made against Burr's character or for expressing any point of view that could be considered "despicable."

Despicable

Synonyms for *despicable* include "hateful," "detestable," "abominable," "awful," "odious," "vile," "low," "mean," "shameful," "shabby," "dirty," "rotten," and "lowdown."

Hamilton's response? *Be more specific.*

The affair of honor was in play.

Burr and Hamilton's seconds did not have a prayer of repairing the rift. Burr's declaration didn't give Van Ness a lot of wiggle room. Hamilton's second, Nathaniel Pendleton, had even less. Hamilton told Pendleton that Burr's letter was "unanswerable."

Past Experience

Over the years, the hotheaded Hamilton had been involved in the first steps leading up to a duel on six other occasions. But he had always been the one demanding an apology for a slight or insult. None of these incidents had progressed beyond the outraged stage. The affair of honor with Burr was different. Hamilton was the one who would have to humble himself, admit wrongdoing, and beg forgiveness.

But he was not that kind of guy.

Hamilton would sooner—and soon—risk everything rather than turn away from Burr's challenge. Hamilton did not believe in dueling. But he did not believe in apologizing to Burr—who gave as good as he got. Backing down would mean disgrace.

The duel was a done deal long before Burr's second knocked on Hamilton's door. Burr had something to prove. Hamilton's prickly personality and history with Burr made him the perfect target. By June 27, their fates were sealed. Usually the actual event would happen quickly. But Hamilton had cases pending in court and didn't want to cause trouble for his clients. The schedule got pushed up to July 11.

Intentions and Preparations

For Hamilton, upholding his honor in an affair of honor meant throwing away his shot. For him, the values that he lived by—that he admired in his greatest mentor, Washington, and had demanded of his lost son—were courage, honesty, virtue, integrity, and a strong moral character. His self-respect depended on nothing less. The few people who knew Hamilton's plan understood his motives, but they simply couldn't believe it. Nothing anyone said could change his mind.

The days leading up to the duel were business as usual. Hamilton and Burr even attended a dinner together to honor Revolutionary war heroes. Hamilton helped his son James with a speech for school. He and Eliza threw a garden party. Not as usual were the papers and letters he prepared in case he didn't survive. Hamilton knew there was a chance he'd be leaving Eliza with many debts and few assets. She and their children would need to get support from her family.

"I am a dead man."

At 5 a.m. on July 11, Hamilton, Pendleton, and Dr. David Hosack rowed across the Hudson to a beach below the Palisades near Weehawken, New Jersey. Hamilton and Pendleton climbed a path to a clearing on a narrow ledge. The seconds prepared the pistols—the same set Philip had used—as Burr and Hamilton took their places ten full paces apart. Hamilton, facing the morning sun sparkling on the river, paused the action. He fetched out his glasses and checked his aim.

Once ready, the seconds turned their backs. (This kept them from seeing anything in case they were asked to testify later.) At Pendleton's command, two shots rang out. The seconds turned as Hamilton crumpled to the ground.

Hosack (also not on the scene to avoid being called as an eyewitness) ran up from the boat to find Pendleton cradling Hamilton in his arms. Hosack was sure Hamilton was already dead and was amazed when he opened his eyes as they crossed back over to Manhattan. Hamilton lived until the following afternoon—long enough to say goodbye to Eliza, to his children, and to his heartbroken family and friends. He was forty-nine years old.

"Best of Wives and Best of Women"

Elizabeth Schuyler Hamilton deserves to be mentioned in the list of extraordinary women whose influence built the new nation. Like Martha Washington and Abigail Adams, Eliza showed the compassionate devotion, fierce loyalty, and generous support that embodied the character and courage of the American spirit. She outlived "her Hamilton" by fifty years, raising his children, preserving his memory, and promoting his legacy.

In her husband's honor, Eliza was a founder and, later, director of the first private orphanage in New York City. She collected Hamilton's papers for publication, along with information from his colleagues and correspondents to clarify details. She and Dolley Madison raised money to build the Washington Monument on the National Mall.

Eliza died in 1854 and was buried next to her husband. She was ninety-seven years old.

In a letter he left for Eliza, Hamilton wrote: "If it had been possible for me to have avoided the interview, my love for you and my precious children would have been alone a decisive motive. But it was not possible, without sacrifices which would have rendered me unworthy of your esteem."

Nathaniel Pendleton later went back to the clearing to find the bullet from Hamilton's pistol. It had smashed into a tree limb, high and wide of the mark.

"My friend, Hamilton, whom I shot."

Many years after the duel, Burr returned to New Jersey and recalled that day. He described hearing Hamilton's bullet zing through the tree branches overhead. His recollection revealed that he knew Hamilton had thrown away his shot. When Burr pulled the trigger, he was shooting to kill.

Burr faced murder charges in New Jersey and New York, but he returned to Washington, D.C. The office of the vice presidency gave him immunity from being prosecuted.

In 1806, Burr was arrested for treason in a plot to take over the Louisiana Purchase and turn it into his own empire. After being acquitted on a technicality, Burr went to Europe. He died in New York in 1836 without ever being tried for the murder of Alexander Hamilton.

A Lasting Legacy

Hamilton's life began under a dark cloud of shame and loss. It ended in a bright flash on a reckless morning. In between—with a combination of luck, courage, diligence, sharp wits, deep love, and fierce loyalty— Hamilton built a life, a family, a career, and a nation. In the process, he forever left his mark on history.

**Monument marking the grave of Alexander Hamilton
at Trinity Church.**

Alexander Hamilton is buried in the Trinity Church
Cemetery, on the corner of Wall Street and Broadway, just steps
from where he worked to create the United States of America.
His epitaph is a tribute to his character and a testament to his
accomplishments.

THE PATRIOT of incorruptible INTEGRITY.
THE SOLDIER of approved VALOUR.
THE STATESMAN of consummate WISDOM;
Whose TALENTS and VIRTUE will be admired
BY
Grateful Posterity
Long after this MARBLE shall have mouldered into
DUST.

Glossary

affair of honor—a challenge to defend one's character in a duel

aide-de-camp—a military officer acting as a trusted assistant to a senior officer

arsenal—a collection of weapons and military equipment stored by a town

Articles of Confederation—the first constitution of the United States

delegates—people sent or authorized to represent others at a meeting or conference

federal—of or relating to the central government of the United States

grapeshot—iron balls a little smaller than golf balls fired from cannons

Loyalists—colonists during the American Revolutionary period who supported the British cause; see *Tories*

mercenaries—professional soldiers hired to serve in a foreign army

militia—a military force made up of the local civilian population to help the regular army in an emergency

monarchy—a form of government with a king or queen at the head; a monarch is the king, queen, or member of the royal family; a monarchist is a person who supports this form of government

mutiny—openly refuse to obey orders given by a person of authority, such as an officer

Parliament—the legislature made up of the monarch, the House of Lords, and the House of Commons in Britain

privateers—armed ships owned by private individuals hired by a government especially in time of war; pirates

ratify—to approve a treaty or agreement

tariffs—charges to be paid for particular imports or exports

Tories—American colonists who supported the British side during the American Revolution; see *Loyalists*

traitor—a person who betrays a friend, country, or principle

treason—the crime of betraying one's country by killing the ruler or overthrowing the government

Bibliography

Brookheiser, Richard. *Alexander Hamilton, American.* New York: Simon & Schuster, 2003.

Chernow, Ron. *Alexander Hamilton.* New York: Penguin, 2004.

Ellis, Joseph J. *The Quartet: Orchestrating the Second American Revolution, 1783–1789.* New York: Knopf, 2015.

Fleming, Thomas. *Duel: Alexander Hamilton, Aaron Burr and the Future of America.* New York: Perseus, 2000.

Flexner, James Thomas. *The Young Hamilton: A Biography.* Boston: Little, Brown, 1978.

Freeman, Joanne B., ed. *The Essential Hamilton: Letters and Other Writings.* New York: Library of America, 2001. [Volume compilation, introduction, notes, chronology, 2017.]

Hamilton, Alexander. *The Papers of Alexander Hamilton,* 27 vols. Harold C. Syrett and Jacob E. Cook, eds. New York: Columbia University Press, 1961–1987. [Online resource: *Founders Online*]

Hamilton, Alexander, James Madison, and John Jay. *The Federalist Papers.* Introduction and commentary by Garry Wills. New York: Bantam, 1982.

Hamilton, John C. *The Life of Alexander Hamilton,* 7 vols. Boston: Houghton, Osgood, 1879 [1841–1864].

McCullough, David. *John Adams.* New York: Simon & Shuster, 2001.

Miranda, Lin-Manuel, and Jeremy McCarter. *Hamilton: The Revolution.* New York: Grand Central Publishing, 2016.

Randall, Willard Sterne. *Alexander Hamilton: A Life.* New York: HarperCollins, 2003.

Risjord, Norman K. "The Compromise of 1790: New Evidence on the Dinner Table Bargain." *The William and Mary Quarterly,* Vol. 33, No. 2 (Apr. 1976), pp. 309–314.

Tucker, Phillip Thomas. *Alexander Hamilton's Revolution: His Vital Role as Washington's Chief of Staff.* New York: Skyhorse, 2017.

Source Notes

The following list identifies the sources of the quoted material found in this book. Note that quotations may retain unconventional spellings and punctuation that reflect the writing of the day.

URLs are provided for quotes from online resources. Complete information on each source can be found in the bibliography.

Abbreviations

AHA—*Alexander Hamilton, American* by Richard Brookheiser
AHRC—*Alexander Hamilton* by Ron Chernow
AHWR—*Alexander Hamilton: A Life* by Willard Sterne Randall
EH—*The Essential Hamilton: Letters and Other Writings*, edited by Joanne Freeman
JA—*John Adams* by David McCullough
LAH—*The Life of Alexander Hamilton* by John C. Hamilton
QJE—*The Quartet: Orchestrating the Second American Revolution, 1783–1789* by Joseph Ellis

Introduction: A Man Named Hamilton

Page 1   "Mine is an odd destiny.": From Alexander Hamilton to Gouverneur Morris, [29 February 1802], *Founders Online*, National Archives, last modified June 29, 2017, founders. archives.gov/documents/Hamilton/01-25-02-0297.

Chapter 1: Beginnings

Page 3   "It seems my birth . . . criticism.": From Alexander Hamilton to William Jackson, 26 August 1800, *Founders Online*, National Archives, last modified June 29, 2017, founders.archives.gov/ documents/Hamilton/01-25-02-0068.

Page 6   "shameless, rude, and ungodly": AHWR p. 14.

Chapter 2: The Counting House

Page 9   "I wish there was a war.": From Alexander Hamilton to Edward Stevens, 11 November 1769, *Founders Online*, National Archives, last modified June 29, 2017, founders.archives.gov/documents/ Hamilton/01-01-02-0002.

Page 16   "I would willingly risk my life . . . my Station.": From Alexander Hamilton to Edward Stevens, 11 November 1769, *Founders Online*, National Archives, last modified June 29, 2017, founders. archives.gov/documents/Hamilton/01-01-02-0002.

Page 17   "Reflect continually . . . you have just made.": From Alexander Hamilton to William Newton, 1 February 177[2], *Founders Online*, National Archives, last modified June 29, 2017, founders. archives.gov/documents/Hamilton/01-01-02-0023.

Page 17   "His cargo was stowed . . . pickledy.": From Alexander Hamilton
           to Henry Cruger, *24 February 1772, Founders Online*, National
           Archives, last modified June 29, 2017, founders.archives.gov/
           documents/Hamilton/01-01-02-0025.

Page 19   *The Hurricane* (excerpt): EH p. 4.

Chapter 3: America

Page 20   "Then join hand in hand . . .": "The Liberty Song" by John
           Dickinson; www.americanrevolution.org/war_songs/warsongs6.
           php.

Chapter 4: Student to Soldier

Page 28   "No man in his senses . . . slave.": EH p. 9.

Page 36   "prove [to be] the salvation . . . liberties.": AHRC p. 55.

Page 37   "venomous brood of scorpions": AHRC p. 58.

Page 38   *A Full Vindication of the Measures of the Congress* (excerpt): EH p. 9.

Page 39   "The sacred rights . . . by mortal power.": AHRC p. 60.

Chapter 5: Revolution!

Page 40   "Are these the men . . . defend America?": From George
           Washington to John Hancock, 16 September 1776, *Founders
           Online*, National Archives, last modified April 12, 2018,
           founders.archives.gov/documents/Washington/03-06-02-0251.

Page 41   "Concord Hymn" by Ralph Waldo Emerson: www.
           poetryfoundation.org/poems/45870/concord-hymn.

Page 42   "What an unfair method of carrying on a war!": AHRC p. 66.

Page 44   "Fly for your lives or anticipate your doom.": AHRC p. 63.

Page 45   "disgrace and injure the glorious cause of Liberty": AHRC p. 64.

Page 46   "In times of such commotion . . . fatal extremes.": From
           Alexander Hamilton to John Jay, 26 November 1775, *Founders
           Online*, National Archives, last modified February 1, 2018,
           founders.archives.gov/documents/Hamilton/01-01-02-0060.

Page 49   "open and avowed rebellion": AHRC p. 67.

Page 49   "with as much unconcern . . . not been there": AHWR p. 98.

Page 54   The Declaration of Independence "In Congress, July 4, 1776 . . .":
           www.archives.gov/founding-docs/declaration-transcript

Page 57   "brilliant courage and admirable skill": AHWR p. 114.

Page 57   "a youth, a mere stripling . . . plaything.": AHWR p. 114.

Chapter 6: Promotion

Page 58   "It is not a common Contest we are Ingaged In.": From George Washington to Brigadier General William Woodford, 3 March 1777, *Founders Online,* National Archives, last modified February 1, 2018, founders.archives.gov/documents/Washington/03-08-02-0533.

Page 58   "We have not slept . . . this place.": AHWR p. 116.

Page 62   "It is a fine fox chase, my boys!": AHRC p. 84.

Page 65   "It is absolutely necessary . . . to find my aides.": AHWR p. 119.

Page 66   "always upon the stretch . . . for recreation": AHWR p. 122.

Page 68   "the hurry of business": AHWR p. 123.

Page 69   "principle and most confidential aide": AHRC p. 91.

Chapter 7: Trials and Tribulations

Page 71   "For Gods sake . . . distress is infinite.": From Alexander Hamilton to Colonel Henry E. Lutterloh, [February 1778], *Founders Online,* National Archives, last modified February 1, 2018, founders.archives.gov/documents/Hamilton/01-01-02-0390.

Page 76   "chased like a covey of partridges": AHRC p. 99.

Page 82   "I now, Sir, in the most explicit terms . . . under him.": From Alexander Hamilton to Major General Israel Putnam, 9 November 1777, *Founders Online,* National Archives, last modified February 1, 2018, founders.archives.gov/documents/Hamilton/01-01-02-0338.

Page 83   "I approve entirely . . . good intentions.": From George Washington to Lieutenant Colonel Alexander Hamilton, 15 November, 1777, *Founders Online*, National Archives, last modified February 1, 2018, founders.archives.gov/documents/Washington/03-12-02-0251.

Chapter 8: Vows and Victories

Page 89   "We have it! We have it!": LAH p. 382.

Page 89   "I am sorry . . . equally essential points.": To Alexander Hamilton from Lieutenant Colonel John Laurens, 18 December 1779, *Founders Online,* National Archives, last modified June 29, 2017, founders.archives.gov/documents/Hamilton/01-02-02-0546.

Page 91   "I leave it to my conduct . . . their friendship.": From Alexander Hamilton to Catherine Schuyler, [14 April 1780], *Founders Online*, National Archives, last modified June 29, 2017, founders.archives.gov/documents/Hamilton/01-02-02-0648.

Page 92   "a poor man's wife . . . examine well your heart.": From

Alexander Hamilton to Elizabeth Schuyler, [August 1780], *Founders Online*, National Archives, last modified June 29, 2017, founders.archives.gov/documents/Hamilton/01-02-02-0834.

Page 97   "I am in very good health . . . my Betsey.": From Alexander Hamilton to Elizabeth Schuyler, [2 October 1780], *Founders Online*, National Archives, last modified June 29, 2017, founders. archives.gov/documents/Hamilton/01-02-02-0884.

Page 98   "Instead of finding the General . . . so we part.": From Alexander Hamilton to Philip Schuyler, 18 February 1781, *Founders Online*, National Archives, last modified June 29, 2017, founders. archives.gov/documents/Hamilton/01-02-02-1089.

Chapter 9: Lawyer and Delegate

Page 105   "We have now happily concluded . . . fruits of it." From Alexander Hamilton to John Jay, [25 July 1783], *Founders Online*, National Archives, last modified April 12, 2018, founders. archives.gov/documents/Hamilton/01-03-02-0270.

Page 110   "The uneasiness . . . fatal effects.": QJE p. 56.

Page 110   "Your Excellency . . . out of confusion.": From Alexander Hamilton to George Washington, [13 February 1783], *Founders Online*, National Archives, last modified June 29, 2017, founders. archives.gov/documents/Hamilton/01-03-02-0155.

Page 110   "lessen the dignity and sully the glory": AHWR, p. 282.

Page 110   "I have not only grown gray . . . my country.": AHRC, p. 179.

Chapter 10: The Power of the Pen

Page 114   "I fear that we shall let slip...anarchy and misery.": Alexander Hamilton to George Washington, [3 July 1787], *Founders Online*, National Archives, last modified June 29, 2017, founders.archives. gov/documents/Hamilton/01-04-02-011.

Page 121   "if I have reason to believe . . . waste of time.": From Alexander Hamilton to George Washington, [3 July 1787], *Founders Online*, National Archives, last modified June 29, 2017, founders. archives.gov/documents/Hamilton/01-04-02-0110.

Page 123   "a commerce so repugnant . . . enlightened people.": Memorial to Abolish the Slave Trade, 13 March 1786, *Founders Online*, National Archives, last modified June 29, 2017, founders. archives.gov/documents/Hamilton/01-03-02-0503.

Page 125   The Preamble to the Constitution: www.archives.gov/founding -docs/constitution.

Page 128   *The Federalist* No. 15 (excerpt): EH p. 119.

Page 129   Federal Ship *Hamilton* banner: AHA p. 74.

Chapter 11: A Member of the Cabinet

Page 130   "the most enlightened friends . . . are the highest": EH p. 174.

Page 130   "It is my great desire . . . on my own farm.": To Alexander Hamilton from George Washington, 28 August 1788, *Founders Online*, National Archives, last modified June 29, 2017, founders.archives.gov/documents/Hamilton/01-05-02-0025.

Page 134   "His Rotundity": AHRC p. 278.

Chapter 12: Decisions and Disgrace

Page 145   "Alas, alas, how weak is human nature.": JA p. 493.

Page 145   "And why can we not have an American bank?": EH p. 66.

Page 147   "the invasions of the legislature": To George Washington from Thomas Jefferson, 15 February 1791, *Founders Online*, National Archives, last modified June 29, 2017, founders.archives.gov/documents/Washington/05-07-02-0207.

Page 156   "Having contributed . . . not a little.": From Alexander Hamilton to Angelica Church, 8 December 1794, *Founders Online*, National Archives, last modified June 29, 2017, founders.archives.gov/documents/Hamilton/01-17-02-0407.

Chapter 13: A Matter of Honor

Page 157   "Every day proves . . . not made for me.": From Alexander Hamilton to Gouverneur Morris, [29 February 1802], *Founders Online,* National Archives, last modified June 29, 2017, founders.archives.gov/documents/Hamilton/01-25-02-0297.

Page 159   "Myself and most . . . in the extreme.": AHWR p. 421.

Page 160   "No one, better . . . greatness of your loss.": From Alexander Hamilton to Martha Washington, 12 January 1800, *Founders Online,* National Archives, last modified June 29, 2017, founders.archives.gov/documents/Hamilton/01-24-02-0140.

Page 162   "Tis not to a Chapter of Accidents . . . of Interest.": From Alexander Hamilton to John Rutledge, Junior, 4 January 1801, *Founders Online*, National Archives, last modified June 29, 2017, founders.archives.gov/documents/Hamilton/01-25-02-0156-0001.

Page 166   "the frail and worthless fabric": From Alexander Hamilton to Gouverneur Morris, [29 February 1802], *Founders Online*, National Archives, last modified June 29, 2017, founders.archives.gov/documents/Hamilton/01-25-02-0297.

Page 168   "unanswerable": AHRC p. 687.

Page 169   "I am a dead man.": AHRC p. 703.

Page 171   "Best of Wives and Best of Women": From Alexander Hamilton to Elizabeth Hamilton, [4 July 1804], *Founders Online*, National Archives, last modified June 29, 2017, founders.archives.gov/documents/Hamilton/01-26-02-0001-0248.

Page 171   "If it had been possible . . . of your esteem.": From Alexander Hamilton to Elizabeth Hamilton, [4 July 1804], *Founders Online*, National Archives, last modified June 29, 2017, founders. archives.gov/documents/Hamilton/01-26-02-0001-0248.

Page 172   "My friend, Hamilton, whom I shot.": AHRC p. 721.

Image Credits

About the Author

SUSAN BLACKABY comes from a family with deep roots in Alexander Hamilton's America and compelling connections to his legacy. About 100 years after Hamilton set up the national banking system, J. R. Blackaby, Susan's great-grandfather, founded the Bank of Jordan Valley in a frontier town in eastern Oregon. And 200 years after Hamilton was appointed secretary of the treasury, her grandfather Earl Blackaby retired from his tenure as city treasurer of Ontario, Oregon, after serving longer than any city treasurer in U.S. history. Susan lives on a bluff overlooking the Columbia River. She writes for young readers almost exclusively, genre-hopping across a wide range of topics. Visit her website at www.susanblackaby.com to learn more.

Index